A DESCRIPTION
of the
QUALIFICATIONS
Necessary to
A GOSPEL MINISTER

A DESCRIPTION
of the
QUALIFICATIONS
Necessary to
A GOSPEL MINISTER

*Advice to Ministers and Elders
Among the People Called Quakers*

by
SAMUEL BOWNAS
(1676-1753)

Pendle Hill Publications and Tract Association of Friends

Philadelphia

A Description of the Qualifications Necessary
to a Gospel Minister *was first printed at the Bible
in George-Yard, London, in 1750, and was reprinted there
in 1767 and 1853. This edition follows the 1767 text,
with slight revisions for modern readability.*

Book Design by Carol Trasatto
Printed in the United States of America
by Thomson-Shore, Inc., Dexter, Michigan

Library of Congress Cataloging-in-Publication Data

Bownas, Samuel, 1676-1753.
    A Description of the qualifications necessary to a gospel minister:
advice to ministers and elders among the people called Quakers /
by Samuel Bownas.
        p.   cm.
    Includes bibliographies.
    ISBN 0-87574-911-9
    1. Society of Friends—Clergy—Early works to 1800.
    2. Clergy—Office— Early works to 1800. 3. Society of
    Friends—Doctrines.
    I. Title.
BX7745.B69 1989
248.8'92—dc19   89-2948
                                                                  CIP

Contents

FOREWORD vii
ACKNOWLEDGMENTS xi
EDITOR'S PREFACE xiii
INTRODUCTION xvii

I

SANCTIFICATION IS A PREVIOUS QUALIFICATION FOR THE
RECEPTION OF A DIVINE INSPIRATION TO MINISTER

3

II

THE NECESSITY OF DIVINE INSPIRATION
TO THE BEING OF A GOSPEL MINISTER,
AND TO CONDUCT HIM IN HIS MINISTRY

15

III

ADVICE TO MINISTERS IN A STATE OF INFANCY

26

IV

ADVICES AS TO THE MATTER AND MANNER OF EXPRESSION

39

V

ADVICES TO A CAUTIOUS CONDUCT AND DEPORTMENT
IN THEIR TRAVELS IN THE WORK OF THE MINISTRY

51

VI

CAUTIONS AGAINST PRIDE AND EXALTEDNESS,
MEDDLING IN MATTERS, SPREADING REPORTS, ETC.,
AND A GENERAL RECOMMENDATION OF HUMILITY
AND MEEKNESS IN ALL THINGS

64

VII

ADVICE TO MINISTERS IN THE STATE OF YOUNG MEN,
WHEREIN SELF-CONCEIT OF THEMSELVES,
AND TOO LOW ESTIMATION OF OTHERS,
MAY BE APT TO RAISE THE MIND ABOVE THE LOW
AND HUMBLE STATE WHEREIN ITS SAFETY ONLY IS

80

VIII

MISCELLANEOUS ADVICES AS TO MARRIAGE,
TRADE, AND AN UNBLAMABLE CONDUCT

90

A SHORT VIEW OF THAT GREAT AND SOLEMN DUTY OF PRAYER

103

Foreword

Mind the Lord, and stand in his will and counsel.
Look not forth at time nor place, but at thy Father's
house, wheresoever thou art. And dwell in the pure
measure of God in thee. . . . For the bringing forth
many out of prison art thou there set; behold, the
Word of the Lord cannot be bound. . . . Dear heart,
be valiant, and mind the pure Spirit of God in thee,
to guide thee up unto God.

> George Fox
> *Epistle 113, To a Friend in the ministry*

We are in a period of change, when some old values are near to being lost. It is vital that Friends take stock of their inheritance, and, looking to their Foundation, realize anew what those strengths were which enabled them to endure many difficulties and gave them an influence far beyond their numbers. The nurture of a vocal ministry which is more than intellectually able — although intellect can have a part in a well-rounded spiritual experience — is a matter of paramount concern if the life within our Society and its impact without are to continue. The nurture of a true gospel ministry is of paramount concern if the great work of carrying the gospel of Jesus to the world, which is the ultimate purpose of all Christian endeavor, is to go forward.

This new publication of an old work, which sets forth ably and fully the nature and practice of true gospel ministry, may help in strengthening and upbuilding a revival today. Not every reader may agree with everything the author has to say, but all will recognize the clear and logical way it is presented, and it will repay thoughtful reading. The publishers hope it may not only help preserve the old values in which the life of the Quaker community is rooted, but show that such values are indeed new, since all truth is timeless: as fresh and meaningful now as when Samuel Bownas journeyed tirelessly to what were then the far places in order to minister to needs there. The far places of today are different from those of the seventeenth century, but there are still far places and there are still the same needs, and a need for a dedicated ministry to meet them.

. . . at the hearing of the speech of the true minister, there is a joy to all that seek and thirst after righteousness; for the preaching the gospel is the glad tidings, the joyful news, and is a comfort to soul, body and spirit, to all that receive it.

George Fox
Epistle 312, On ministry in worship

The cooperation of Pendle Hill and the Tract Association in preparing this work for publication is a new departure which we feel is a sign of healthy growth in our Society. The interrelation of different groups with differing directions and emphases may well lead mutually to the strengthening of their work and the enrichment of all.

The advice and assistance of all whose efforts and lively concern have contributed to this publication are deeply appreciated by the Tract Association of Friends.

JAMES DEANE
TRACT ASSOCIATION OF FRIENDS

ACKNOWLEDGMENTS

This book owes its appearance ultimately to the deep reservoir of "gospel life" from which Samuel Bownas, the minister, originally drew. To those who have tasted enough of this spiritual refreshment to encourage and enable the present publication as a testimony to the ultimate authority of God, we are grateful.

The teaching of William Taber and Sandra Cronk in classes at Pendle Hill drew seekers who wanted to read more of Samuel Bownas's work. The Tract Association of Friends has for many years faithfully reprinted the work of early Friends who can still answer to the seeking of modern Friends. Pendle Hill's publications committee recognized the value of a joint publication arising out of such deeply mutual concerns.

James Deane of the Tract Association and William Taber of Pendle Hill agreed to write the foreword and introduction respectively. Cate Van Meter and Rebecca Mays of Pendle Hill joined with Patrick Burns of the Tract Association to begin editorial work. Gay Nicholson of Pendle Hill ably completed the editorial work and oversaw production of the volume.

Editor's Preface

This volume of Samuel Bownas's *A Description of the Qualifications Necessary to a Gospel Minister* is a revised reprint of an early edition, published in 1767. Work proceeded from a fragile original copy which resides in the Pendle Hill library, and editorial decisions were guided by a single purpose: enhanced readability for a late twentieth-century audience.

Capitalization of common nouns has been eliminated, and italicization retained only when serving the modern function of special emphasis. British spellings have been retained, since they are familiar to most readers of the English language.

Eighteenth-century punctuation has been streamlined. Very lengthy sentences have, where possible without altering meaning, been broken up around appropriate clauses; in some of these cases, conjunctions have been deleted. An inconsistently applied system of topic enumeration has been eliminated.

Verb forms have been modernized, except in biblical quotations: for example, *findest* becomes *finds; administerest* becomes *administers*; *saith* becomes *said*. For reasons of consistency and euphony, the nominative *thou* has been replaced with *thee*. Thus, "thou art clear" becomes not "thou are clear" but rather "thee is clear."

Traditional usage of masculine pronouns and terms has been retained, but Bownas's meaning should not be misconstrued. The careful reader will note that Samuel Bownas did use gender-inclusive language, though inconsistently. We know that he was indeed writing for both women and men as equally apt recipients of the gift of gospel ministry.

The many biblical quotations have been made precisely consistent with the King James Version, which Samuel Bownas would have known and used. Where obvious paraphrases or references occur and are not noted in the original, citations have been added. However, biblical language pervades the entire work. The reader is encouraged to cultivate an appreciation such as biblically steeped eighteenth-century Friends would have possessed for the depth of Samuel Bownas's connection to the scriptural tradition.

Qualifications remains, as the publishers intended, essentially unaltered as an eighteenth-century work. Modern literary sensibilities may render Samuel Bownas's style grandiloquent, his construction awkwardly repetitive and roundabout. The reader is thus encouraged to meet Bownas in his own literary world by adopting a slowed, meditative pace. With this adjustment, the rich language can be savored, and the periodic sentences allowed to build like a series of waves to the fullness of each point.

Through each of the many readings required to edit this work faithfully, I have experienced not tedium or saturation, but rather a fresh invitation to enter still more deeply into the living tradition Samuel Bownas describes. The reader is similarly invited.

GAY NICHOLSON
PENDLE HILL PUBLICATIONS

INTRODUCTION

In the last few years a number of Friends have rediscovered the little book by Samuel Bownas which has had an important influence on Quaker ministers since its first publication in 1750. Bownas's description of the ideal development of a Quaker minister seems especially relevant in these closing years of the twentieth century when so many Friends are digging deep for a fresh understanding of our roots. Since most of the surviving volumes can be found only in rare Quaker libraries, people have had to make do with photocopies, as have students in my classes about Quaker ministry at Pendle Hill and Haddonfield (N.J.) Monthly Meeting. The enthusiasm of these students and the hunger of many Friends for more readily available resources from our spiritual heritage led to this revised reprint.

The first few pages of this introduction are intended to make a bridge between the world of Samuel Bownas and the modern Quaker reader. The remainder points to the story of his life as a good example of what he tried to teach Friends about ministry.

Because Samuel Bownas's eighteenth-century world was — in some ways — so different from our own, the modern reader will find it helpful to read this book on several levels. The first level involves a sympathetic understanding of the evolving Quaker culture which Samuel Bownas experienced and was trying to edify. The second level involves sympathetic attention to an important part of that culture — its theology and language. Some readers who might otherwise be offended or turned away by Bownas's Christian and biblical language may be helped by understanding that he, like George Fox, saw Quakerism as a rediscovery of original Christianity, or to use a modern term, "alternative Christianity." It was a rediscovery not only in terms of outward ethical practice, but also in terms of theology and states of consciousness. Bownas's use of this traditional language grows out of Fox's illuminating way of expanding and explaining orthodox Christian language in his *Journal* and other writings.[1] Finally, the third level of reading involves a more meditative process of identifying Bownas's practical spiritual wisdom, which

[1]The content of Chapter IV, "Advices as to the matter and manner of expression," suggests that biblical themes and allusions were a substantial part of eighteenth-century Quaker ministry.

can apply to the nurture and support of a living ministry in our own time.

From the very beginning, Friends have recognized that some women and men are especially called and gifted in the vocal ministry. When George Fox died in 1691, and Samuel Bownas was only fifteen years old, the Quaker system of ministry had already been firmly established and would continue, with only minor changes and adjustments, past the middle of the nineteenth century. Fox had urged that ministers, when traveling to visit other meetings, should carry some sort of credential from their monthly meetings. This custom still survives in what is called a *traveling minute*. In his lifetime, British Quakers were *recorded* or recognized as a minister by being present at the Second Day meeting of ministers in London, and after 1724 by action of their monthly meeting. In North America, the responsibility for authenticating and recording the minister was assumed by monthly meetings at an earlier date.

After 1860, the system began to evolve into the pastoral or programmed tradition among large groups of North American Quakers. London Yearly Meeting ceased to record ministers after 1924, hoping to lay the responsibility for ministry more broadly upon the entire membership. Most unprogrammed Friends around the world have also given up the practice of recording — or they never had it, as in the case of the newer yearly meetings. Here and there in North America, it is still possible to find a modern unprogrammed Friend who has been recorded as a minister. Even so, the old system has changed so much in the twentieth century that only among a few pockets of Conservative Friends would Samuel Bownas now recognize the style of ministry familiar to him. In recent years there has been a growing interest in recovering the power which Quaker ministry once had, and a few people, often younger Friends, have once again begun to feel called into traveling ministry, home visitation, and "opportunities," all of which were common among Friends before the twentieth century, and have never entirely disappeared.

When the young Samuel Bownas spoke his first words in meeting a few years after George Fox's death, he took the first outward step in the classic development of a Quaker minister, but he had already experienced the all-important inward qualification. *Qualification*, as he uses the word, implies that one has gone through a process of personal transformation which reorients the ego, the will, and the attention so that one can be trusted purely to receive and purely to give forth an inspired message. Bownas insists that a substantive transformation should occur before real ministry can begin, or as William Penn said of early Friends, "They were changed men themselves before they sought to change others." He describes this transformed state with a term which may be difficult for some modern Friends: *sanctification*. Actually, anyone who has been moved to pick up this book has probably already experienced some measure or glimmering of sanctification, as in those moments when we have a new clarity, a new freedom to, in John Woolman's words, "turn all that we possess into the channel of universal love." However, we must not gloss over the fact that Bownas uses *sanctification* in a biblical and Christian context, and that this first step towards the ministry is usually preceded by a difficult and sometimes anguished struggle, often described in the early pages of journals written by Quaker ministers.

Most twentieth-century unprogrammed Friends are shy about saying that we are sanctified or even that we have fully passed through the purging, ego-altering fires of personal transformation. "If this be the requirement," we would say, "who dare speak in our meetings?" In this uncomfortable place Samuel Bownas can help modern Friends who minister in meeting to ponder if there are indeed deeper places from which ministry can flow, if there are indeed yet deeper levels of self-knowledge and yet deeper levels of pure attentiveness beyond the reach of the ego's hidden agenda.

A careful, sympathetic reading of Bownas's book and some Quaker journals[2] can gradually help a modern Friend begin to sense the difference between ministry that flows only from the intellect or from the emotions, and ministry that wells up from a deeper source. Similarly, such painful pondering can lead Friends to recognize that sometimes our speaking in meeting is partly to convince and convert ourselves, and that sometimes such speaking might be more appropriate in a gathering other than meeting for worship.

It is almost as if, in the late twentieth century, Bownas's first qualification does not tend to occur *before* one speaks in meeting, but rather stretches out over a number of years, gradually transforming and eventually bringing that person's life and spoken ministry to a deeper level. However, the classic convincement and transformation experience does still happen to some modern Friends before they ever speak in meeting, and we can assume that this will continue to be the case, perhaps increasingly so as the current wave of renewal deepens.

A second qualification Bownas describes results from the belief that ministers' outward style of living should bear witness to their inward transformation, a belief which later re-

[2]See Howard H. Brinton, *Quaker Journals: Varieties of Religious Experience Among Friends*. Pendle Hill Publications, 1972.

sulted in the retention of archaic patterns of dress and behavior. Some modern readers may find Bownas a bit strident or old-fashioned on this point, until we realize that he is simply saying that the inward must always bear fruit in the outward. Even in our hurried era, might we listen more readily to a man here or a woman there who seems to have achieved a serenity and a visible integrity of life which give power to their words?

The second chapter and much of the rest of the book deal with the third fundamental qualification for Quaker ministry which is made possible by the preceding two. This is the ability to know when one is called to speak and when one must remain silent, so that ministry comes from the Spirit rather than from some other source. Here it is especially important to recognize how different Bownas's Quaker culture was from ours. For example, in his time few people spoke in meeting except recorded ministers or those who were moving toward becoming recorded. Such ministers were experienced in discerning the difference between a true inward *motion* to speak and a mere *notion* to speak, or they were rapidly gaining such experience, and they could expect to be *eldered* (cautioned or corrected) if they strayed too far from this qualification. Experienced ministers might have spoken hundreds of times in scores of different places in Great Britain and North

America, preaching sermons that were much longer than we could tolerate today. They set a high standard for anyone else who felt led to speak in meeting.

In our time, on the other hand, many more people take occasional responsibility for the ministry, but there are relatively few ministers who have gone through the long and arduous experience of learning by discerning that was typical of most ministers (sometimes called *public Friends*) of the eighteenth century. Perhaps thoughtful readers of this book may find insight into how, in our very different circumstances, we can develop the kind of nurture and fellowship which would help the growth of such experienced, discerning, dedicated ministry, so that it may once again flourish among us.

Samuel Bownas saw the long process of learning and growing in this third qualification as being divided into roughly three stages: the state of infancy in the ministry, the state of young man in the ministry, and the state of father in the ministry. As he describes growth on this path and offers practical advice for each stage, it again becomes clear how different his world was from ours. Yet, allowing for all these differences — concerning marriage customs, for example — the system of Quaker ministry that he describes still has a strong appeal for many Friends who long for its renewal in ways appropriate for our very different time. As we look to such a renewal, it is well to remember that the system he describes was never perfect and that it was constantly evolving. If it had been perfect, Samuel Bownas would not have written this book![3]

As Bownas's description of the gradual qualification or apprenticeship proceeds, the modern reader becomes aware of one significant difference between the system of Quaker ministry then and now. To be a Quaker minister then meant that one had accepted a vocation, a calling, which was more important than one's economic vocation and which often determined it or frequently interrupted it, as was true with Samuel Bownas. After becoming recorded, the minister's apprenticeship became even more arduous and time-consuming than before. For one thing, there were more meetings to attend. Ministers and elders usually had to attend special meetings on the monthly, quarterly, and yearly meeting levels, and they

---

[3]It is instructive to see how many of Bownas's ideas about the nurture and behavior of ministers can be found in London Yearly Meeting's first printed discipline, which appeared in 1783. A "between the lines" reading suggests that there had always been some traveling ministers who were insensitive or who abused the hospitality which was offered as a matter of course. As more people become led to travel in the ministry in our time, it is well to consider how modern Friends can also develop clear accountability and "quality control" of those who undertake this very important work.

felt a responsibility to attend the regular business meetings also. Travel to all of these meetings involved considerable time and often expense as well. A very real expense, especially for those who traveled some distance to yearly meeting or traveled for months or years at a time in ministry, was the time lost from productive economic activity. The "training" went on for a lifetime, even as already long experienced ministers traveled in pairs or with an elder, and as they visited with each other for counsel, encouragement, and spiritual refreshment. In this craft and vocation the Quaker minister was both very much alone and at the same time encouraged and sustained by a religious society which believed that God does indeed raise up individuals with a special gift and calling in the ministry.

◆

Samuel Bownas's life, which is summarized in the next few pages, is a good example of the kind of minister he describes in this book: a person who is called and transformed, who begins his ministry cautiously and gradually, who is responsive and obedient to wiser and more experienced Friends, and who devotes literally years of his life to his first vocation, ministry. Yet even when he becomes a "father" in the ministry, he remains a humble member of the body of Christ, speaking only as he is led. And he earns his own living, even paying most of his own expenses while traveling.

By the time he wrote *A Description of the Qualifications Necessary to a Gospel Minister,* Samuel Bownas had long been regarded as a "weighty" and gifted minister in North America and the British Isles, but, as he tells in his published journal,[4] he entered adulthood as a "traditional Quaker" who needed to be awakened by a traveling minister, just as he himself would later awaken hundreds of other people into new life. A second generation Friend, he was born in 1676 at Shap, Westmoreland, while the Society was still struggling for its life under Charles II. His father, who had been persecuted for holding meetings in his own home, died soon after Samuel's birth, leaving the small family so poor that Samuel's schooling ended when he was ten, old enough to tend sheep. At thirteen he was apprenticed to blacksmiths, first to an uncle who was unkind to him and then to Samuel Parat, near Sedburgh in Yorkshire, whom Samuel describes as "a very honest Friend." As a child Samuel had heard stories about his father's faithfulness. He had witnessed persecution when he and his mother worshiped with Friends locked outside their

[4]*An Account of the Life, Travels, and Christian Experiences in the Work of the Ministry of Samuel Bownas.* London, 1756.

meetinghouse, and visited Friends in prison. Yet, in spite of this background, he began his apprenticeship as a young man who "had no taste of religion, but devoted myself to pleasure," even though he dressed and spoke in the plain Quaker way. He did go to Brigflatts Meeting, where he spent most of his time sleeping.

Samuel records in his journal that at a First Day meeting in late 1696,

> . . . a young woman, named Anne Wilson, was there and preached; she was very zealous, and fixing my eye upon her, she with a great zeal pointed her finger at me, uttering these words with much power: "A traditional Quaker, thou comest to meeting as thou went from it (the last time) and goes from it as thou came to it, but art no better for thy coming; what wilt thou do in the end?" This was so pat to my then condition, that, like Saul, I was smitten to the ground, as it might be said, but turning my thoughts inward, in secret I cried, "Lord, what shall I do to help it?" and a voice as it were spoke in my heart saying, "Look unto me, and I will help thee;" and I found much comfort, that made me shed abundance of tears. (5)

After this meeting the change in his life was remarkable:

> I longed for the meeting-day, and thought it a very long week. When the time of meeting

xxviii

came, my mind was soon fixed and staid upon God, and I found an uncommon enjoyment that gave me great satisfaction, my understanding being opened, and all the faculties of my mind so quick, that I seemed another man. (6)

Suddenly, he found new levels of understanding about the Bible which had been "as a sealed book to me," about preaching "in the power and the Spirit," and about the enormous difference between a Quakerism "only by education" and a Quakerism truly alive to the Spirit.

Within just a few weeks, he spoke in meeting for the first time, beginning what he would later describe as his "infancy" in the ministry. His journal describes, with refreshing honesty, some of the details of this infancy and of the help and counsel he received from older Friends and fellow infants. By 1698, at the age of twenty-two, he set off walking toward Scotland on his first ministerial journey, carrying his traveling minute from the monthly meeting, which was by that time required of all traveling ministers. Then he felt led to buy a horse and to travel as a minister through much of England. After his first journey he no longer had a home or regular employment, but he sometimes stayed long enough in one place to earn enough money for clothing and necessities, usually from work during the harvest season.

By the time he made a second journey to Scotland in 1701, he was already an experienced and well-regarded young minister, having passed through many trials, described or alluded to in his journal, which later helped him to be a psychologically perceptive mentor to young and infant ministers. Throughout his journal, but especially in these early years, he records many examples of how older and more experienced Friends encouraged and counseled him along the way. From his account it is clear that even though the Religious Society of Friends was then scarcely fifty years old, there was already a significant unwritten "science" about Spirit-guided ministry which experienced ministers and elders gladly passed on to the young men and women who were being called to it.

Elders were gradually assuming more and more responsibility for the nurture and care of all ministers, especially the young ones. Although there had been unofficial elders from the earliest years of the Society of Friends, they now began to be officially appointed to attend the special meetings of ministers to give advice and counsel as needed. Just as ministers were seen as having a special gift and calling, elders were seen as having a special gift of spiritual discernment, a strong sense of the Quaker tradition, and a gift for encouraging others in their spiritual growth. Although *Qualifications* was written primarily for young and infant ministers, it is also full of advice for those who would nurture them.

One example of Samuel's trust in more experienced Friends occurred after his young fellow minister Isaac Alexander was sent home by the elders at Bristol for his hard preaching and repeated prophecies of "a great mortality" to come there. Isaac accepted his treatment with humility, went home and continued to grow as a minister, because, said Bownas, young Isaac had humbly remained in unity with Friends. When Isaac had a concern to travel in the ministry again, his meeting would not grant him a traveling minute until they had received written clearness from Bristol Friends, who eventually wrote to say that he was "a sincere young man who intended very well, and they were glad he took their admonition right," and that they were comfortable for him to resume travel in the ministry. In the meantime, Samuel Bownas had begun to feel a similar concern to prophesy about a great mortality in the city of London. However, after he had traveled to London, he called together a small group of experienced Friends to ask their advice before he allowed himself to preach on the subject that was burning within him. They listened with great tenderness as he explained how Isaac's concern had been quashed by Bristol Friends and how he had then taken up the same concern. After a time of quiet, they gently told Samuel their sense that he was probably more influenced by his love for his friend Isaac than by the Holy Spirit. They did not, however, forbid him to preach; they simply advised him to wait, for if his concern were truly from God, it would grow stronger; if not, it would decrease. And so it proved; the concern gradually went away, and Samuel and Isaac were both much wiser ministers and more kindly spiritual guides because they themselves had been treated with such tenderness.

By 1699 or 1700, "a young woman, who afterwards became my wife, had strong hold of my affections," but they did not marry until after Samuel had journeyed in Scotland in 1701 and in North America from 1702 to 1706. As he set out across the Atlantic at the age of twenty-six, he was already an authoritative and much-traveled minister who had spoken in hundreds of meetings, many of them specially appointed at his request. Before sailing, he wrote a letter of advice to the Kendal meeting of ministers. The letter reveals that he was already a keen observer of the ministry of others and was beginning his lifelong service as a teacher and minister to his fellow ministers. As he modestly wrote in his journal, this letter was "the first fruits of that kind to my brethren." Many of the topics he would develop in *Qualifications* are already touched upon.

During four years of travel, Samuel visited virtually every colonial Friends meeting at least once, if not several times. The vigor of his ministry among Friends and non-Friends on Long Island caused him to be imprisoned for almost a year at the instigation of George Keith, a contentious Quaker who had become an Anglican priest. In prison, Samuel used his time well, conversing with many people who came to see him. He also learned to make shoes, and made them so well and rapidly that he earned enough money to pay his prison expenses, as well as the expenses of the next stage of the journey.

In the Dover area in New England, Samuel felt a powerful concern to gather ministers together in a meeting which was a foretaste of many later meetings in which he would have very perceptive, very specific messages for fellow ministers. In this case,

> some of them were got into an extreme of preaching and praying, and would continue meetings to an unseasonable length, as likewise in their preaching and praying at table. . . . They themselves say they were wrong in doing as they had done, and got out of this extreme, which was a degree of ranterism. (99)

Upon his return to England in 1706 he and his wife-to-be went through the steps preceding a Quaker marriage. For Samuel this meant returning to his home meeting in the north, where he turned in his traveling certificate (still the custom today) and reported on his travels to the monthly meeting. Then he asked for a certificate of his clearness for marriage. On the journey back to the south for the wedding he was accompanied by "my worthy friend James Wilson," with whom he visited meetings along the way. Again we see Samuel as a mentor of other ministers: "I found my companion under a great concern to speak something in meetings, but very backward and reluctant to give up to it, but I gave him encouragement such as I was able." When James ran into discouragement in the large Bristol meetings, Samuel "cheered him up as well as I could, by giving him an account of my experiences, and when we came to the little country meetings again, he did finely, and gathered strength and experience in the work very fast."

Following the convention of most Quaker journal writers, Samuel did not say much about his marriage and family life, but what he did say makes it very clear that he loved his wife and deeply treasured their life together until her death in 1719. He also treasured the friendship of many of the ministers with whom he traveled or who came to visit him. Scattered references in other Quaker journals make it clear how much other ministers valued his friendship and spiritual support.

By the time of his second marriage to "the widow Nichols" in 1722, he had begun to record other occasions when he spoke with authority as a teacher to his fellow ministers, and he had noted several times the danger of a formal, plain Quakerism which by-passed the need for inward rebirth and purging from pride.

When the fifty-year-old Samuel Bownas made his second journey to North America in 1726, he must have been in his prime as a minister, as described in Joseph Besse's preface to his published journal:

> His conversation was free, generous and affable; neither did he shun the society of those whom he was sent to convert. . . . He was of a grave deportment, and of a tall, comely and manly aspect. His public preaching was attended with such a divine authority and majestic innocence, as commended the attention of his hearers; and his voice being clear, strong and distinct, was capable of conveying his profitable exhortations to the ears and understandings of a very numerous auditory. (vi)

In eighteen months he traveled some 5,322 miles through heat and bitter cold, visiting most meetings from two to six times, missing only seven "far back in the woods." In the twenty years since his previous visit, Quakerism in North America had greatly expanded; he counted fifty-six new meeting-houses and many enlarged ones, but he was greatly concerned that young Friends were growing up into a formal Quakerism and that they were not so alive spiritually as the previous generation. Clearly, he had become what he describes in *Qualifications* as a "parent" in the ministry, for he gave long messages to the meetings of ministers and elders in many places. The fact that these meetings were unusually well-attended, even by ministers and elders from other places, suggests that Samuel's teaching ministry to ministers and elders was much valued. His occasional journal record of these meetings contains much of the subject matter and many of the expressions which later appear in *Qualifications*.

After his return to wife and home in 1728, he went on no major journeys until 1740, though he certainly attended and probably often preached at neighboring monthly meetings, quarterly meetings, and at yearly meeting. Apparently he devoted enough attention to business during these years so that a 1738 letter could describe him as

> a wealthy merchant out of Dorsetshire, a punctual payer of the King's duties, and a detester of the smuggling trade. He delivers vast quantities of excellent goods, gives large measure and good pennyworth. It is said he was a blacksmith somewhere about Sedburgh in his

young years, not then worth five pounds per annum, but I really think he has been at the university since he left the anvil, for even while he is expressing his traffic he talks like a philosopher and returns as much in a week as some do in seven years. He is now very able and rides like a Parliament man.[5]

This evidence of the respect and prosperity he had earned as a merchant makes an interesting commentary on the careful advice he gives to ministers engaged in business in *Qualifications*. Like so many others in the 350-year succession of Quaker ministers, he had observed that faithful ministers almost always developed a "competency," a means of employment which made it financially possible to leave home for long periods of time. Samuel's competency was substantial enough that he could write, two years before his death, that he then had an income of forty pounds a year, quite adequate for that time and place.

When he felt a renewed call to travel in 1740, he continued to be given a special ministry in meetings of ministers and elders, as well as in the regular meetings. During the three months he was in Ireland, he attended about eighty-two meetings. He cut short further visits because of his wife's illness in the latter part of 1740.

[5]David Hall to James Wilson, 4 mo. 24, 1738, Skipton, Yorkshire. Alfred Rodman Hussey Collection, Haverford College.

He recorded no more visits until after her death in 1746. Then, for the next three years, he made more visits, though his journal now records fewer details as his energy and power fail. To the very end he had messages for other ministers, as in the Second Day morning meeting for ministers just after the 1740 London Yearly Meeting: "I was much drawn forth to the ministers, the meeting being very large with country Friends."

As his powerful ministry to ministers was drawing to a close, *Qualifications* was published in 1750, when he was seventy-four years old. No doubt Friends had long encouraged him to put his insights about ministry into writing. After 1749 he had quit writing in his journal, for his hands shook and his eyes were weak. Yet he continued to attend his own and neighboring meetings as long as possible, and Friends remembered that "his ministry was lively and powerful to the last, to the edification and comfort of those that were favored with it." (197-198)

WILLIAM P. TABER, JR.

A DESCRIPTION
of the
QUALIFICATIONS
Necessary to
A GOSPEL MINISTER

CHAPTER I

As THE DESIGN of the following pages is to set in a true light the nature and necessity of an inspired ministry, and the advantages that we receive thereby, I shall, as introductory thereunto, briefly take notice of a qualification suitable to the receiving of that inspiration, without which it is not reasonable to suppose anyone to have it.

There must be a state of <u>sanctification</u> (in degree) known, by the spirit of judgment and burning, before any can be proper objects to be receivers of this inspiring gift, that can only assist a minister and make him* instrumental of doing good to others. The tree must be good before the fruit can be so; and right and true ministers are to be known by their fruits. This being granted, which I think can't be denied, then it follows that none, without being thus qualified, can be called to the work of the ministry by a divine inspiration of the Holy Spirit;

*See Editor's Preface regarding masculine pronouns and terms.

3

and therefore all vile and ungodly persons, while they continue in that natural and unregenerate state, are excluded from any part in this gift. Although some such may pretend that either with their learning or by their money, or both, they may have acquired or made a purchase of orders for liberty to preach, and may on this foundation undertake to expose what they have to sell; but what they sell is no other than what they have bought while in this unregenerate state, empty and vain, and cannot profit the hearers. For as the Psalmist says, "Unto the wicked God saith, What hast thou to do to declare my statutes, or that thou shouldst take my covenant in thy mouth? Seeing thou hatest instruction, and casteth my Ps 50:16-17 words behind thee." Let me say that whosoever undertakes the work of the ministry, not being first reformed themselves, cannot justly expect to be inspired by divine wisdom for the reforming others by the Word of Truth; for she dwells in holy souls, and makes them friends of God and prophets. Then it is reasonable to conclude that all who live in "adultery, fornication, uncleanness, lasciviousness, idolatry, witchcraft, hatred, variance, emulations, wrath, strife, seditions, heresies, envyings, murders, drunken-

Gal 5:19-21 ness, revellings" and such like works of the flesh are excluded from any inheritance in the kingdom of God, and consequently from having any part in that excellent inspiring gift of

4

the ministry, so necessary to our assistance and direction in our way thither.

I shall therefore say something of the qualification necessary to receiving of this excellent inspiring gift of the ministry; and in order to it, we ought first to examine our own hearts with care, praying in secret that God, by his Spirit, will vouchsafe to direct us in a right search after truth. Hereby we shall find a law in our hearts that we have broken, and a Spirit in our inward parts that we have rebelled against, and in our ignorance, being hurried in the pursuit of the pleasures of the flesh and vanities of this life, have overlooked, though we have been followed by it, and it has strove with us. For the Spirit works in us secretly, and we know not at the first what it is; but finding ourselves very uneasy and in great trouble of mind, being under sorrow and heaviness, not rightly and coolly examining the reason, it is often mistaken to proceed from a natural cause. And so outward means are sought for to relieve from this uneasiness; some by taking their bottle with their companions, others diverting themselves with their sports and gaming, others taking medicines to help them against what they call melancholy; some one way and some another thus mistake and make merry over the witness in them, and stiffen their necks against the reproof of instruction, which is the way to

5

life; not minding the text, which says, "He, that being often reproved hardeneth his neck, shall suddenly be destroyed, and that without remedy."

Prv 29:1

But though some are thus rebellious and careless, others take a better course, by strictly examining their words and actions, company and conversation, and finding it to be their great sorrow and burden, instead of endeavouring to get from under the load of trouble by sporting, gaming, drinking, medicine, or company, such rather, as the Prophet said, sit alone and keep silence, putting their mouth in the dust, praying in secret that God will assist them by his grace and good Spirit, that the cause of this sorrow may be removed by an humble and sincere repentance of all their follies and sins, wherewith they have offended God, and that for time to come, they may by the help of the Spirit and direction of that law in their hearts, which they had hitherto overlooked and neglected, now lead a new life; by denying all ungodliness, and abstaining from every appearance of evil, which must be done before they can perfectly practice that which is right in the sight of God. For no man can be righteous and wicked at one time; we must first be brought out of the bondage of corruption under spiritual Pharaoh and Egypt, into the wilderness, before we can offer acceptably unto God.

Cf.
Lam 3:28-29

6

This state is figuratively called a wilderness, a way we have not trod in, showing thereby the necessity of depending on our guide, our spiritual Moses, that must go before and take care of our support. For in this wilderness state we have no food, no water, no right refreshment but what this our leader provides and administers to us. In this state we can neither pray nor do any religious act without the direction of our leader, so that we find the case is much altered with us to what it was in time past. For then we could pray, sing, preach, and perform other religious duties in our own time, feeding and satisfying ourselves therewith, but now we are brought into the wilderness, where there is neither ploughing nor sowing. We can't now help ourselves by our own contrivance, and workings in our own wills, but here we must live a life of faith, wholly depending on him that will (if we faint not in our minds) bring us through to the heavenly Canaan. Thus we shall come in the Lord's time to experience the substance of those types and figures, under that legal dispensation to be substantially and spiritually fulfilled in our own minds by the operation of the Spirit of our Lord Jesus Christ, the substance and foundation of all true religion and ministry that is really profitable to the hearers.

This work of preparation by the Spirit being thus begun and carried on, is a shorter or longer time in accomplishing, so as the parties thereby may be qualified to receive a divine inspiration to minister from to others, according to the will of him that calls. And when it happens to be but a short time between persons beginning to be serious and religious, and the time that they appear in the ministry (labouring according as they apprehend themselves to be called to that work for the good of others), it may happen that some of their hearers, forming their judgment respecting the worthiness or unworthiness of the parties so concerned from their past conduct, while in so vile a state, may conclude, "How can such be fit to teach others, who themselves but the other day were guilty of such follies as are inconsistent with a true minister to touch with?"

Thus in some respect it was with that great apostle of the Gentiles, Saul, afterwards Paul. For we find, while he was in the very heat of persecuting the church and breathing out threatenings against the brethren, so that they were afraid of him; as Ananias was when commanded of the Lord, during that peculiar visitation which at that time he was under, to go to his assistance; Ananias's answer was, "Lord, I have heard by many of this man, how much evil he hath done to thy saints at Jerusalem, and here he hath authority from the chief priests to bind all that call on thy name. But the Lord said unto him, Go thy way: for he is a chosen vessel unto me." Then Ananias went, having this special command to visit Saul. But it plainly appears that this good man could not easily believe Saul's so sudden and short change from an open opposer and persecutor of the faith, and faithful professors and followers of the Son of God, to be an open professor and preacher of the same faith and doctrine with them he so persecuted. And as this was the case of Saul, it has been the case, in some degree, of others of later date; that is, their sudden change, from a vain conversation to be preachers against it, has so narrowed up their way in the minds of some of their hearers that at the same time, some of them (that have wished well to the cause of religion), supposing such preachers would be a means of stumbling to many, have therefore in a zeal that has been without true consideration and right judgment, not giving time for trial whether what they have heard was of God or the creature, (as not minding Gamaliel's counsel) been for pulling them down before they could see whether they were right or wrong.

Acts 9:13-15

Cf.
Acts 5:34-39

To prevent this rash judging, it is needful that the hearers be careful to judge nothing before its time, but let every such person have the opportunity to make full proof of their ministry, that it may appear whether what they do in the way of ministering be of God or of themselves. If it be right, it will be self-evident, and carry with it that which in time will give satisfaction to those who have doubted of the ministry of such persons, and their hearts will be filled with charity towards them.

Now if we consider the thing right, this rash judging is very dangerous and hurtful, greatly tending to the discouraging of young ministers. For this censorious and critical temper is a great block in the way, and may hinder some from coming forth in that gift, though they may be rightly concerned therein; and some that may make a little appearance that way may be put to silence before they have had time sufficient to make or to give full proof of their ministry. This temper therefore ought carefully to be watched against, and have a timely curb and discouragement in every mind. Every hearer ought in fear to request of God to be directed aright in judgment, that under a pretended care to promote the cause of religion, they may not in a blind zeal be instrumental to discourage so useful a gift.

Now we find this critical temper, that was so apt to judge without judgment and to find fault without cause, our Lord did frequently reprove when it appeared, as may be seen in the instance of the woman, whose penitence and humiliation induced her to wash her Master's feet with her tears, and wipe them with her hair. Whose Cf. Lk 7:37-38 demonstration of love to our blessed Lord (when Simon was ready to censure him for admitting) he by a very lively comparison commended, and in the application thereof smartly reproved the want of judgment as well as charity of that Pharisee, who did so little for him himself, and yet was so ready to find fault with her; and by that means rather brought him to justify what he had before condemned. Which is often the case of self-righteous professors, who are so apt (without just and mature consideration) to judge those who from vile and ungodly sinners may suddenly become purified by the work of the Spirit, and by the same may be fitted and required (though some may be apt to think it too soon) to come up in public service for God; while themselves, who have not loved so much, not been so zealous to follow divine conviction, are lingering behind in the work. Yet these are most apt and ready to judge and censure those who are more faithful, and thus suddenly brought into obedience, as too hasty and forward.

And also in his answer to those who censured him for eating and drinking with publicans and sinners, he plainly declared the end of his coming, which was the reason of his conduct in that as well as other respects.

From all which it appears that it has happened sometimes, the more vile and wicked anyone has been before conviction, the more thorough and quick has their conversion been. They to whom much is forgiven *love much;* and the more they love, the more hearty and zealous they are to go on with the work unto which they are called; and having known the terrors of the Almighty for sin, are the more earnest to persuade men. And I dare not say but that such may in their zeal and warmth of spirit a little stretch, at times beyond their authority; but when they do, they no sooner retire to their gifts but they find sufficient smart for it in their own minds. But this begets them enemies; and because they appear wrong in *part,* they must by some be concluded wrong in the *whole;* which is an unwarrantable conclusion to make on any person.

Now if we rightly consider the matter, there may be a just cause for this zeal, if we will but give them this allowance: that as they have been like brands plucked out of the burning, and known the terrors of the Almighty for sin, they are the more earnest to persuade men to repentance and amendment, both by reproof, warning of sinners, and threatening them with judgment, as having themselves so narrowly escaped. This being the cause of that fervour and zeal such have appeared in, it will no doubt on strict examination be found that the root of all this is love, and a design of good to the souls of men. Such therefore ought to be treated with great charity and meekness, and the good design in them encouraged; and that over-forwardness in them rather shown to them than reproved. And when they see it, they will not need to be told of it, for shame will come fast enough upon them (if they are true ministers), and may lie heavy; which may hinder some tender spirits from improving in their gifts, and render them less serviceable than otherwise they might, if they did moderately keep on their way, minding to keep pace with their gifts, neither going before nor staying behind their leader. But wanting both judgment and experience, being children in the work, they can't do it all at once, and therefore in patience must be borne with for a time.

This preparation by the Spirit for the ministry so qualifies the receiver of this excellent inspiring gift, when called to the work, that he can experimentally say, "What I have tasted, felt, and heard of the good Word of Life, and the powers of the world to come, I declare unto you." But what can such (as the Apostle speaks of, concerning whom he declares they shall not inherit God's kingdom) say of their experience of the work of God's power in them, while they continue in their gainsaying in the works of the flesh, such as adultery, idolatry, pride, covetousness, envy, and drunkenness, minding the pleasures of this world above anything else? Surely (as above) they have no experience to speak of to the people, nothing to say that will bring them to a fellowship with the Father and his son Jesus Christ.

Having said thus much concerning a true qualification for the receiving of this gift of inspiration, so absolutely necessary to every right minister that without it he cannot be one, I shall now speak of inspiration itself, which is to be the subject next in course to be treated of, concluding this chapter with part of that excellent prayer of David's (so apt to this purpose) in the fifty-first Psalm, from the ninth to the thirteenth verse. "Hide thy face from my sins, and blot out all mine iniquities. Create in me a clean heart, O God; and renew a right spirit within me. Cast me not away from thy presence; and take not thy Holy Spirit from me. Restore unto me the joy of thy salvation; and uphold me with thy free Spirit. Then will I teach *(but not till then)* transgressors thy ways, and sinners shall be converted unto thee." A short but full description of the right qualification of a gospel minister.

CHAPTER II

Having said so much of the needful qualification in order to be inspired by the Holy Spirit, and enabled thereby to minister good to others, it is necessary also to say something of inspiration itself, which is by many too much exploded, and slighted as a thing at an end, and long since ceased. They suppose all things needful for instruction to piety and virtue already revealed in that excellent book called the Bible, which I prefer to all books extant, and request the diligent reading thereof with due attention and regard to what the Apostle says of them: "All Scripture is given by inspiration of God, and is profitable for doctrine, for reproof, for correction, for instruction in righteousness," and able to make wise to salvation through faith in Jesus Christ. Now it is this faith in Christ which makes the Scriptures really and truly profitable; but a man without this faith may read the Scriptures until he has them by rote, and can repeat a great part of what he has so often read; and yet receive no profit from them. For as holy men wrote them by inspiration of the Spirit, so by it we

2 Tm 3:16

15

must come to a right understanding of them; otherwise they will be as a book sealed, and the bare reading of the letter will be no other than a bare report of things at a distance. For when we read the words of Moses, that he spoke in the ears of Israel, importing that "thou need not say in thy heart, who shall ascend into heaven, or go beyond the sea," we find that to fetch the word of command he would not have them look at a distance for it, because (adds he) "it is nigh in thy heart and mouth."

Cf.
Dt 30:12-14

Now the Apostle, expounding the words of Moses, says, "But the righteousness which is of faith speaketh on this wise, say not in thine heart, Who shall ascend into heaven? (that is, to bring Christ down from above:) Or, Who shall descend into the deep? (that is, to bring Christ up again from the dead.) But what saith it? The Word is nigh thee, even in thy mouth, and in thy heart: that is, the Word of Faith, which we preach." Now this Word that is in the heart and mouth of inspired ministers is that by which they must be acted, if they do right in the work of the ministry; and indeed, unless this Word in the heart opens the understanding, there can be no right preaching. It is true, men may by study and frequent reading acquire to themselves a form of words, and frame a set and studied speech in a regular way, methodically dividing and subdividing their

Rom 10:6-8

matter,* raising uses and applications from the present subject before them. All this may be done by the man, the creature, and natural part, having nothing of inspiration or power of the Spirit in it. And pray, what will this ministry do for the hearers? It comes from the head, and the contrivance of the man's part; therefore it can reach no further; for no stream can arise higher than its fountain. And that ministry which is of man, though it may be very pleasing to the creature and acceptable to the itching ears, who with the Greeks of old seek after wisdom but not that which is from above, is not profitable to the hearers. For the Jews sought after a sign, and the Greeks after wisdom, but neglected the preaching of Christ crucified and risen from the dead as foolish doctrine and not worth their regard. But unto as many as believed in the Word preached by the inspiration of the Spirit, they found it to be (both Jews and Greeks) the mighty power of God to salvation. Now that which made this spiritual ministry so profitable to them that received this doctrine is the very same that makes the Scriptures profitable to those who rightly read them, namely, faith in Christ, who is the living Word and light of men; which Word is preached by every true minister inspired thereunto by the Spirit of Truth.

*We would say "subject matter" today.

17

Now this inspiration ought to be rightly understood and believed in. From my own experience I understand it to be an *inbreathing* of the divine Word into our minds, giving a true understanding of divine things, that we may make choice of and walk in the paths of wisdom, which is the just man's path. I say, the inbreathing of this Word, which is truth, life, and the light of men; that Spirit which "searcheth all

1 Cor 2:10

things, yea, the deep things of God," which by Jesus Christ is made manifest unto all men, ought to be waited for in all our religious assemblies especially, and believed in, as being the foundation and spring of all right ministry, devotion, and worship of the true God. Yea, I always find this, from my own experience, to be most edifying, thus to wait for this divine inspiration in all our religious assemblies. And when I find my understanding inspired and influenced by this blessed gift to minister to others, I give up thereto, speaking to the assembly according to the present ability received

Cf.
1 Pt 4:11

thereby. I know this to be the true beginning of a right gospel ministry, which I shall speak to more at large in its proper place.

Now, I understand by the inbreathing of the Spirit of Christ into our minds thus much: namely, as the Apostle asserts, "We know that the Son of God is come," and for proof adds

1 Jn 5:20

that he "hath given us an understanding." This

18

was to themselves undeniable. But what means the Apostle by saying, "He has given us an understanding?" He can mean no other than a *spiritual* one. For they doubtless had understandings as natural men before; but by that natural understanding they could not perceive the things of the Spirit of God, nor comprehend the light which shined in darkness; which is still the same, even until now. But the true knowledge of the coming of the Son of God in Spirit and power is by inspiration from heaven, or the revelation of the Father by the Son; and this is the foundation of the true church and ministry, against which no opposition can ever prevail. By this understanding, they knew him that is true, and were in him; and so must all true believers experience the same, if true members of Christ's church, and ministers of his Word. I say, this spiritual understanding, which they received by revelation, was an undeniable evidence to them, and so it is to us. But how shall I prove this to a demonstration, to such as are in a natural and unenlightened state, that I have this revelation and am thus inspired?

Answer: It is not possible to do it, until they who are in unbelief come to believe in the same power, and receive inspiration by the same Spirit, to give them a right knowledge of the things of God. For the natural man receives

Cf.
1 Cor 2:14
them not, because they are foolishness unto him; neither can he in this state know them. This makes it highly necessary for all that profess faith in Christ to apply themselves to God for the gift of his Holy Spirit; for, says our blessed Lord, "Which of you having a son, if he ask bread, will give him a stone?" And thus applies it: "If ye then, being evil, know how to give good gifts unto your children, how much more shall your heavenly Father give the Holy Spirit to them that ask him? Ask and it

Cf.
Lk 11:9-13
shall be given you." What greater encouragement can be given to us than this? It is therefore greatly to be desired that all people, especially such as profess faith in Christ, would in humility and godly sincerity ask of God a portion of this Spirit, whereby we may know the things of God. For it is this Spirit, which is the "Com-

Jn 14:16
forter" that our blessed Lord promised to pray the Father to send in his name, which, when we receive, will lead us into all truth. This is that Spirit that will reprove the world of sin, because they believe not in the only begotten Son of God. This is that Spirit which gives life, and will make thee a living member of the true church. If thee is devoted in thy mind to follow it, thee will become fruitful in religion, and thy faith will be both living and powerful in thee, to give victory over the world, that natural part in thee that would not submit to the testimony of Jesus, nor believe in the only begotten Son of God.

20

I say then, inspiration or revelation from God by his Spirit is of absolute necessity to guide a minister in his ministry. A minister so conducted by a gospel power and light, inspiring his mind with the *how* and the *what* he shall say, will speak with the Spirit, and understanding also; that is, he will understand by his own experience the work of the Spirit, and Word of Faith in his own mind, and that what he says is true. And although he has this experience, as above, yet it is not meet for anyone, in his own time and will, to speak thereof in an assembly; but we are to wait for both authority and power, that in the Lord's time we may speak (of what our eyes have seen, our hands handled, and what we have felt of the good Word of Life, and powers of the world to come) to the people with the same view as the primitive Christians did, that is, to bring their hearers into a right fellowship with the Father and his Son our dear Lord and Saviour Jesus Christ. So shall they be one with all that truly believe in him.

But some may object that we may be deceived by supposing ourselves inspired when we are not; and that we have a revelation when it is nothing but an imagination and delusion. In such a state a man may be deceived himself, and all who think of him as he does of himself will in like manner be deceived, and how shall this be avoided?

21

Answer: It is granted, some have been deceived themselves, and have also deceived others, but the cause of this deception is in themselves, for want of an humble waiting to know what they are about; for a true inspiration from God is as plainly to be distinguished from the pretended false one as light is from darkness. For divine inspiration quiets the mind under all opposition and contradiction, and gives power over the world and the lusts of the flesh, and works the redemption of such as are endued therewith and are subject to it. These are very humble and low of heart, and the more their minds are enlightened by divine inspiration, the more they see a necessity to watch over themselves, so that the innocence, meekness, and humility suiting a true and right minister will appear in all their conduct. Such are slow to speak, and ready to hear and receive instruction, and are known by them that are spiritual to be such.

But they who conceive themselves to be inspired when they are not, supposing they have a revelation when it is nothing but an imagination of their own brain, are exalted in their minds, being very heady and stubborn, slighting instruction; more apt to teach than learn, being swift to speak but slow to hear; judging everybody that will not receive them as true ministers by foretelling the ruin and downfall of all their opposers; working themselves up

22

to a strange degree of imagination, endeavouring to drive all before them; and such as will neither hear nor heed what they say, they will be apt to call for vengeance from heaven upon such who offer to oppose them. This, and much more that might be mentioned, is the conduct of these deceived and deluded souls.

Now this error by the party thus deluded might be easily discerned, if they would but give themselves time to think and consider aright in coolness, and desire that the Lord would show them the right way. Here is therefore great need to be cautious and try the Spirit; that is, not to receive anything for inspiration or revelation without being well satisfied in thyself that it is such. This cautious fear will not be displeasing to God, but thee will find thy doubts removed, and thee will be confirmed that what thee has is of God, and will stand. This agrees with the practice of Moses and Gideon, and with what the Apostle advised: "Believe not every spirit, but try the spirits whether they are of God: because many false prophets are gone out into the world. . . . They are of the world: therefore speak they of the world, and the world heareth them. We are of God: he that knoweth God heareth us; he that is not of God heareth not us. Hereby know we the Spirit of Truth, and the spirit of error."

1 Jn 4:1,5-6

23

But supposing I or any other may be inspired, as is aforesaid, from a right spirit. How shall proof be made thereof to another, that he may receive our word that we have by revelation, and not as our word only, but as given us of God?

Answer: In this thee will find no hard task with thy brethren, if thee will but do thy endeavour to live according to that doctrine given thee to preach to others, in the first place. And next, mind that thee, without being inspired, undertake not this work of preaching, neither in thy own time nor will, nor by thy own contrivance, collecting what thee shall say. For by so doing thee will be at a loss and confounded in thyself, and give great occasion of offence to them that hear thee; not only to them that are unacquainted with the gift and unbelievers therein (for they will see that thee is wrong), but thy own brethren will be greatly loaded and uneasy with thy so appearing. For they will soon find that thee is out of thy place in speaking, it not being from inspiration, but an imagination of thy own brain. For "the ear trieth words, as the mouth tasteth meat;" and those who are spiritual will see where thee is, better than thee thyself.

Jb 34:3

But it will be a hard task to make proof of thy ministry, though thee speak as the oracle of God, and minister of that ability which God gives, to such as are in unbelief, and in a state of nature. For the natural man, says Paul, "receiveth not the things of the Spirit of God: for they are foolishness unto him: neither can he know them, because they are spiritually discerned." I say, therefore, it will be impossible 1 Cor 2:14 that such unbelievers, or those in a state of nature (while they are in that state and unbelief) should receive thy word, not as thy word only, but as given to thee of God; because they believe no such thing concerning any man. If therefore thee seems to them as a babbler, be not discouraged; Paul was so accounted before thee. Yet, however, though some may so look upon thee, others may perhaps be reached by thy word. As thee ministers from a right spirit, and keeps in thy gift, thee may be instrumental to beget faith in them that believe not, and greatly to edify and confirm them who believe, so that they'll soon conclude thee is a right minister, not of the letter, but of the Spirit. And thy brethren who are spiritual will give thee encouragement to go on, having fellowship with thee in thy gift as a right minister, approved by them as appointed of God for that work unto which thee is called. For no man ought to take his honour unto himself by any human or external call, until he is called of God, as was Aaron.

I now shall come to speak of the gift itself.

CHAPTER III

"There are diversities of gifts, but the same Spirit.

There are differences of administrations, but the
1 Cor 12:4-5   *same Lord."*

E VERY GIFT OF GOD is from the one and
the same Spirit of Truth that is come by
Jesus Christ; for which reason, though we may
seem to differ in our gifts one from another,
yet the design and end is the same. The same
Spirit as in one, so in all, assisting to that end
which is to turn people from darkness to light,
from the power of Satan to God, that they may
be edified in the true gospel, receiving a remis-
sion of their sins, and an assurance of an inheritance among them that are sanctified through
faith in the only begotten Son of God.

Now there must be some time to gain experience and understanding before anyone can
come to a settlement, and true and perfect
knowledge of his own gift. And want of a right
settlement and true knowledge of this gift, and
keeping to it and in it, is the cause of many of
the mistakes that are committed in the exercise
of it. Thus we ought to consider the ministry

26

in these three states: Infancy. A young man's state. The father's state.

A state of infancy ought to be looked upon with great allowance of charity, and if anything appears manly in such a state, that ought not to be made the standard of others to walk by. We must attribute it rather to the giver than the instrument, that gives to everyone as he will, to some a greater and to others a smaller portion of his Spirit, but to everyone, both preachers and hearers, such a manifestation thereof as by faithful obedience thereto they may profit by it. But the gift of the ministry is our present subject.

Then as to the state of infancy in the ministry, let it be considered that the ministry is a birth. And when anyone at first comes under the exercise hereof, he will find a great perturbation in himself, the cause of which he may be as great a stranger to as Samuel was to the voice of God in the temple, who being called the third time, was at length informed by Eli how to answer. So have some, both young men and women, done of later date, that is, applied themselves to such as they have apprehended had more experience of the work of the Lord than themselves, and after all have found it very hard to give up to the heavenly vision. And when they have given up, it has been in so much weakness

Cf.
1 Sm 3:3-10

and fear, yea, sometimes confusion, that they have hardly known themselves what they have said. If in such a state anyone should overrun, miss in expression, or appear in a behaviour not so agreeable to the minds of their brethren, let such brethren exercise charity. See to thy own gift, thee that is a hearer, and try by virtue thereof whether thee finds not something of God in this infant minister to answer his gift in thy own mind. And if on such a search thee finds not that satisfaction thee desires, yet as it is not proper to lay sudden hands on anyone to set them up, so neither be thee rash to pull them down, but give time for proof, and consider the patience of the husbandman, how he waits for a crop after the seed is sown. Having said so much to the hearer, let me now advise this infant minister.

I know thee will find very hard work in thyself; thy heart will be often very heavy and sorrowful, and in great fear and weakness thee will appear as a minister. It may be much against thy will to appear as such; yea, thee may perhaps dearly repent that ever thee gave up to this service, and more especially if thee answers not thy expectation, which I may venture to say, none at all times do. But as thee keeps humble and low, being honestly given up to be and do just what the Lord by his Spirit would have thee, resignation to the will of God being absolutely necessary for a minister to come to; and as thee gets here, patiently waiting the Lord's time, thee will find a greater degree of excellency by the Spirit to enlarge thy understanding in divine openings. When this grows upon thee, beware of pride and self-conceit, for that has ruined many. But give the honour hereof where due; and the more thee is enlarged, labour to be the more humble, and in so doing thee will find safety.

But under these various trials in thyself, I advise to an inward waiting upon thy gift, to feel the moving thereof in thy own mind, which will by a gentle illumination clear thy understanding and judgment, whereby thee will see thy place and service in the church. And if thee finds it thy place to minister to others, be willing to do thy Master's will, and stand up in the meekness of the Spirit which moves on thy mind, and speak the word thereof according to the present opening that is before thee. Regard strictly on the one hand, by speaking too fast and too loud, thee doesn't overrun thy natural strength, gift, and opening, which if thee happens to fall into, it will bring thee into confusion, and thee will not know when to conclude, and so may shut up thy own way in the minds of thy brethren, and bring thyself under a just censure. Therefore whenever it happens so with thee, *sit down;* for by endeavouring to mend it, thee may make it worse. So on the other hand, be not too low, nor too slow in thy speech, so as to lose the matter that way; but carefully keep to thy opening, avoiding both the extremes. Stand up in a calm and quiet frame of mind, as free as possible from either a fear or care how thee shall come off; but follow thy guide in all circumspection and humility, beginning, going on, and concluding in thy gift. Thus will thee experience what the wise man said to be true: "A man's gift maketh room for him, and bringeth him before great men."

Prv 18:16

Now the state I have considered this infant minister in is such as requires help by tender advice from faithful Friends of experience, so that I may compare him to a babe that wants both the breast and nursing, which should be tenderly and with great care administered. If he be corrected, let it be in love; if encouraged, let it be with prudence. Both may hurt him, if not well timed, and given discreetly.

But now we will suppose him a little grown, and to know himself better than a babe can, in which condition he will meet with exercises according to his growth and experience, against which it's needful to be prepared and watchful. After thee begins to know and see a little where thee is, and what thee is about, there will be an observing eye in thee to look at the exercises and ministry of others, and an aptness to compare thyself with others, which may have some ill effects upon thee if not prudently guarded against. For if thee apprehends on such a view that thy gift excels and is preferable to some others, this may lift thee up and prove hurtful; so on the other hand, if thy brother's gift in thy thoughts is more desirable and acceptable, this may cast thee down, and beget too mean an opinion in thee of thy own gift.

If thee looks out at the excellency and beauty of another's gift to be more than what is in thy own, a desire may arise in thee to render thyself like him, and so endeavour to mimic and imitate the delivery, accent and manner of others. Thus leaving thy own gift, and devoting thyself to follow or be guided by others, thee will soon be under a cloud, and lay a stumbling block in thy own way, and shut up the hearts of thy brethren towards thee. To prevent which thee must consider that as there are diversities of gifts, but the same Spirit, therefore mind thy own gift and not another's, and regard the Spirit that moves thee in it, that being the same that is in thy brother or sister. If thee keeps thy place therein, thee will likewise see that though thy gift is different from theirs, it is the same Spirit. So the administration (or delivery thereof) differs, but it is the same Lord that makes thee to differ from them, and them to differ from thee. Therefore let not the seeming excellency that appears in another's gift above thy own tempt thee to an imitation of either delivery, manner, or accent, lest thee insensibly fall into that theft against which the Lord by his prophet complains, "I am against the prophets . . . that steal my words everyone from his neighbour." Besides, the way thee hereby takes to get credit, and a place in the church, will be the shortest way to lose it, and at best thee will be taken for one that apes and mimics what thee can never attain to. The more thee strives this way, the worse it will be. Therefore I advise thee, keep to thy own gift, manner of delivery, and the matter that is opened in thy mind by the Spirit.

Jer 23:30

To make this point yet more plain, it is needful thee first learn to know there are diversities of gifts, and though thine may differ from another's, yet mind to keep to it. And by this thee will know that thee is in thy gift: if after thee has been exercised therein, thee feels inward satisfaction and comfort to flow in thy mind. But if thee finds trouble and heaviness, consider whether thee has not been out of thy place in the manner of delivering thyself, which relates to the administration, which may justly differ and yet have a beauty in it, though thee may not see it thyself. Or it may relate to the

32

matter delivered, and though that may differ from that of another whose doctrine thee may think more acceptable and in more apt terms, which may tempt thee to imitate him, this will bring an uneasiness and a cloud over thy mind. Therefore keep to thy own way, both in thy opening and delivering thereof, guarding against all affected tones of singing or sighing, and drawing out thy words and sentences beyond their due length, and by speaking too much in a breath and so adding an *ah!* to the end of them, and drawing thy breath with such a force and groan as will drown thy matter, and render thee unacceptable to thy hearers. Likewise guard against superfluous words, impertinently brought in, such as "I may say"; "As it were"; "All and everyone"; "Dear Friends"; and "Friendly people"; with sundry others of the like kind which add nothing to thy matter, spoiling its coherence and beauty of expression. Likewise avoid all indecent gestures of the body, as throwing thy arm abroad and lifting up thy eyes, such gestures not suiting the dignity of the ministry. Neither lift up thy voice beyond thy natural strength, nor strain thyself beyond due bounds, vainly supposing that when thee makes most noise with an accent and tone that pleases thy own imagination, that the power is most with thee; when indeed it is nothing but the heat of thy own spirit, and sparks of thy own kindling, which whoever are overtaken by and give way to must expect no less than to lie down in sorrow.

I therefore advise thee to wait for the descending of the gift of the Spirit, which will bring an exercise over thy mind in which thee may be opened with some matter suiting the present occasion. And when thee finds it is thy place to speak, *stand up;* for it is not to be supposed that all thee may have to say on this or that subject can come before thee begins to speak. And if thee should suppose it and so wait, endeavouring to prepare thyself like a school boy, thee will be greatly disappointed, not speaking what thee intended, but something else that thee intended not, which may be thy trouble and grief. Therefore, when thee finds a subject brought before thee, be not desirous of anything more than the virtue of the Spirit of Wisdom to direct thy mind in rightly dividing the Word; carefully observing, as aforesaid, to stand up with a calm and undisturbed mind. For if thee is under a fear in thyself, of either the assembly or anyone in it, it will much hurt thy service; thy understanding will not be clear. Therefore it is better thee should wait until thee gets over that fearful temper; and thy gift will help thee over this weakness in due time, as thee in sincerity keeps to it. Neither suffer thyself to think of doing something extraordinary to be admired, nor have a desire to appear when it is thy place to be silent, but remember at first it was a cross to speak; let it not be so to be silent. In a true resignation be contented to be just what the gift assists and helps thee to be at that time.

And, being thus prepared, mind the time of thy offering, that thee might not hinder the service of another, nor hurt thy own, by either standing up too soon or standing too long; all which will be prevented as thee keeps in a quiet cool frame, retaining thy understanding, that thee may speak with the Spirit and understanding also. Thus all will be comforted and edified together, and thee will find it most safe to begin and go on in thy ministry. Just as thy strength in the gift is upon thee, so will thy matter and voice be filled with divine virtue and power, and thy hearers will be confirmed that thee speaks by authority from above. Herein will thy joy be very great.

But this resignation spoken of is such that we should be always under, still submitting to the gift; so that if we find some divine openings in our minds which may be intended by the giver for our own instruction, when we find it so, beware of giving that to others which is designed for ourselves. Let us entreat the Divine Being to assist us, by his grace, to make a right application of such openings; and this will still add to our qualification and improvement in the work. But if for want of this care to know thy place, thee should attempt to preach when it is thy place to be silent from the opening aforesaid, thee will by so doing give that away to others which thee ought to feed upon thyself, and so become a formal and unprofitable minister. The true knowledge of the time when to speak and when to be silent (so needful to the very being of a minister) will be lost, and thy labour will be in the dark, and weakness will surround thee on every side.

When thee finds it thy place to speak, begin as if thee were going to relate any matter of fact to a single person, taking care at least, however, not to appear in a more unbecoming manner in an assembly than thee does in thy common affairs. But some have in their ministry delivered themselves more awkwardly and unbecomingly than at other times. Not that I would be supposed to conclude any should, in the same manner and accent, deliver his ministry as his common discourse; but then the difference should be that he should deliver his ministry with more awfulness pertinent to the subject before him than he does his discourse in common, according to the degree of assistance received by the Spirit at that time. And this will be a confirmation to them that hear: that such speak as having authority. But a deportment different from this, and appearing in terms not agreeable to sound doctrine, gives reason justly to suspect the contrary. Such bring contempt upon themselves, being looked on as no other than pretenders to what they have no right to meddle with; besides, to impute such conduct to inspiration still adds to and heightens the offence. Therefore to avoid these faults, begin with temper in coolness of mind, and go on as thee sees thy way open, and finds thy understanding enlarged. Thus will thee have pertinent words to express, and Scriptures which will suit thy matter, and confirm it, will be brought to thy remembrance that may not have been thought of, nor read by thee, long before. Here thee will see a reason for what thee says, thy understanding being clear and bright; thee will be able to render a reason for what thee has preached for doctrine. And if thee should not in thy words exactly suit with the sense of some that are thy elders, yet this friendly, cool temper of mind will render thee open to receive from some kind Aquilla or Priscilla instruction in the way of the Lord more perfectly, all which will end to thy advantage and improvement. Besides, this calm and easy going on in thy delivery will give thee an advantage to raise thy voice, as thee finds inward strength and virtue from the Spirit to increase; and as that grows upon thee, thee will find thy voice to alter and fill with

Cf.
Acts 18:26

virtue, and thy delivery beautified with an acceptable mien and deportment. Thus will thy words be filled with Spirit and life. But if thee raises thy voice higher and speaks faster than thee finds spiritual strength to assist, thee will overrun thy opening, and natural strength also, and unavoidably fall into confusion. Therefore, as thy gift differs from thy brother's or sister's, so may thy delivery, and thy opening also, which I beseech thee to keep to. Then will thee acquit thyself as a man of God, a workman that need not to be ashamed, rightly dividing the Word of Truth. This brings me to speak more particularly to the difference of the operation or opening, being the last head under the Apostle's notice.

CHAPTER IV

*"There are diversities of operations, but it is the
same God that worketh all in all."*   1 Cor 12:6

THIS RELATES TO the opening, which
may likewise differ in the manner of its
being expressed, seeing there are sundry ways
of expressing the same thing.

  ✒ By parables, or comparisons suitably adapted.

  ✒ By allegories.

By parables is the beauty, excellency, and virtue
of truth often set forth in lively and moving
terms, producing in the hearers the passions of
sorrow, anger, or joy, as the matter set forth
affects them, so that hereby they are drawn
unawares to pass a severe judgment upon their
own doings, as in the case of David, when
Nathan had by a parable set forth the rich man's
injustice in taking away the poor man's ewe-
lamb, which was his all, to entertain his guest
with, and thereby sparing his own flock. Now
David, hearing this so movingly described, was
struck with such an abhorrence of so vile an
act that he said, "As the Lord liveth, the man

that hath done this thing shall surely die: and he shall restore the lamb fourfold . . . because he had no pity." Nathan made the application, and said to David, "Thou art the man." And David soon was sensible he had passed a just judgment upon himself. Sundry examples might be brought to set this way of speaking in a true light, but to avoid prolixity, I confine myself to only three more.

Cf.
2 Sm 12:1-7

The first is in Isaiah, where God sets forth the house of Israel under the parable of a vineyard, and the men of Judah as his pleasant plants. Having bestowed great husbandry on the vineyard, he looked for fruit agreeable thereto, but being disappointed, he thus complains, "When I looked for grapes," (meaning thereby the fruits of righteousness, judgment and truth, agreeable to the law of that just God from whom they had received so many and unparalleled favours) "they brought forth wild grapes." Meaning thereby oppression, cruelty, disobedience and injustice, such fruits as the Gentiles (who had not been favoured like the Jews) brought forth agreeable to the nature of their degenerate and corrupt hearts.

Cf.
Is 5:4

The second parable is our Saviour's, wherein he sets forth the injustice of the Jews by the same kind of figure. There was a certain householder who planted a vineyard and let it out

40

to husbandmen, and when the time of fruit came, he sent his servants, whom they beat; he sent again and again his servants, and they met with the same treatment. But at last he said, "I will send my son; perhaps they will show reverence unto him." But instead of that, say they, "This is the heir, come let us kill him, and the inheritance will be ours." This so pricked the Jews to the heart that they soon perceived it related to them, and were sore offended with it.

Cf.
Mt 21:33-38

The third and last that I shall observe here is in Luke 8. A sower, says our Saviour, went forth to sow seed. Some fell by the wayside, and it was trodden down, and the fowls of the air devoured it. Some fell upon a rock, and it withered away, because it lacked moisture. And some fell among thorns, and the thorns sprung up with it and choked it. Some fell on good ground, and brought forth some an hundredfold, some sixty, and some thirty.

Cf.
Mt 13:3-8

These, with sundry others of the like kind interspersed here and there in the text, show the wonderful excellency and beauty which are given to and opened in a minister by the divine Word in speaking by parables, comparisons, or allegories, thereby gaining great attention; and it is very moving and of good service to them that hear, being given and opened by the

Spirit alone. And for this reason thee may be tempted to imitate; which when anyone undertakes who is not qualified nor opened by the Spirit therein, makes confused work; and instead of edifying the hearers, grieves and loads them with trouble and sorrow, to hear solid and divine truths so darkened and perplexed by multiplying words without true knowledge; thus religious people are grieved. But on the other hand, this makes diversion and sport for the looser sort, who are too apt to make a mock at all religion and preaching; for which reason it behooves everyone to consider how they are qualified for the work of the ministry, lest by undertaking what is above their capacities and present strength, they should cause laughter and lightness by delivering impertinent parables, comparisons, and allegories not opened to them nor given them by the Spirit of God; that Spirit which "searcheth all things, yea, the deep things of God," and is the foundation of all the true ministry and ministers.

1 Cor 2:10

By allegories, as the Apostle says: "For it is written, that Abraham had two sons, the one by a bondmaid, the other by a freewoman. But he who was of the bondwoman was born after the flesh: but he of the freewoman was by promise. Which things are an allegory: for these are the two covenants. . . . For this Agar is Mount Sinai in Arabia, and answereth to

Jerusalem which now is, and is in bondage with her children. But Jerusalem which is above is free, which is the mother of us all" (meaning Gal 4:22-26 true believers) that are become the sons of God by faith in Jesus Christ. For none ever received him by faith, but with him they did receive power to become freeborn children of the new Jerusalem. Another of this kind is in Hebrews 7, touching the priesthood, and office of our Saviour as the high priest of our profession and ministry, from whom we are to receive power for that work.

There are yet other ways of the operations of the gift to be spoke to, which to be more intelligible in, I conclude them under the following heads:

- By narration of God's dealing with his people in past ages.

- By recounting the goodness of God to ourselves.

- By declaring the great encouragement we have to virtue, from the blessings that others have met with.

- By expatiating on some particular text.

- By setting forth the sundry dispensations of God to mankind, by opening the mystery of the law that came by Moses as figurative of the gospel, and how the prophets did point at the same thing.

By narration of God's dealing with his people in past ages. Such was the sermon of Stephen, Acts 7, and of Paul, Acts 13, both which have the same tendency. In that of Stephen, the first part of what he said was, by enumerating God's dealings with Abraham, with Isaac, and with Israel, to gain the attention and notice of his hearers. For the substance of that sermon was to let them see they were acted by the same spirit as were their forefathers who stoned the prophets, and put them to death. For (says he) "Ye do always resist the Holy Ghost: as your fathers did, so do ye." This so pricked and galled them that they verified his words, stoning him until he died. By this we may learn the way of the Spirit, which sometimes leads into and opens in our minds matter which only serves to gain upon the affection and attention of them that hear. For if one should fall directly upon their present states without a parable, comparison, allegory, or historical relation as introductory thereto, it might render our labour useless and ineffectual. But such an introduction, given us by the Spirit, may make way for a more searching and close ministry, in setting the states of the hearers in a true light before their eyes.

44

By recounting the goodness of God to ourselves, in his great mercy visiting our souls while in the full career of disobedience. This requires great care and caution, that boasting may be excluded, and the honour of his name, whom we preach, be exalted in our ministry, confirming the same by Scripture, and the experience of holy men recorded therein. Such was that of Paul before Festus and King Agrippa. "Having therefore obtained the help of God, I continue unto this day, witnessing both to small and great . . . that Christ should suffer, and that he should be the first that should rise from the dead. . . . " So that when Paul appealed to the king's faith, urging, "I know that thou believest," he confessed himself, "Almost thou persuadest me to be a Christian." Thus Paul magnified the goodness of God to himself, yet set forth therein that Christ is the true and proper object of faith.

Cf.
Acts 26:22-28

By declaring the great encouragement we have to pursue virtue, from the blessings that others have met with thereby, such as Enoch, Noah, Abraham, Joseph, Samuel, David, etc. The author to the Hebrews, in the eleventh chapter, gives us a large account of the faithfulness of the faithful, both men and women, enumerated to this very end (as himself declares): that we may be provoked by the strongest examples and inducements to follow the same steps in our

45

pursuit of virtue. For when he sums up the evidence (as it may be properly termed) in the twelfth chapter, he begins, "Wherefore seeing we also are compassed about with so great a cloud of witnesses, let us lay aside every weight, and the sin which doth so easily beset us, and let us run with patience the race that is set before us."

Heb 12:1

By expatiating on some particular text in the openings of life, which is still for procuring to them who hear the same end, by begetting faith in Christ the saviour of the world; for faith comes by hearing with a believing heart. Such therefore was the preaching of Philip to the Eunuch, Acts 8. For it is written, "Philip opened his mouth, and began at the same Scripture, and preached unto him Jesus." And somewhat like unto this is that of our Saviour in Luke 4, where " . . . he went into the synagogue on the sabbath day, and stood up for to read. And there was delivered unto him the book of the prophet Esaias. And when he had opened the book, he found the place where it was written, The Spirit of the Lord is upon me. . . . And he closed the book, and gave it again to the minister, and sat down. And the eyes of all them that were in the synagogue were fastened on him. And he began to say unto them, This day is this Scripture fulfilled in your ears," proceeding to the amazement of them that heard him.

Acts 8:35

Lk 4:16-21

46

Lastly, *by setting forth the sundry dispensations of God to mankind, as to Abraham and Lot; and in opening the mystery of the law that came by Moses,* as only preparatory to the gospel, and how the prophets did point out Christ the substance, which was figured forth by the offerings and shadows under that dispensation. Now we find the dispensation of angels to Noah, Abraham, and Lot agreeing with the prophets that came after; for unto Abraham was promised the blessing of all nations. Likewise opening the true and spiritual meaning of Israel's travels, after their being delivered from Pharaoh's power and thraldom, and showing by the Spirit that these things in the history have a meaning to believers in the mystery, such as their going through the Red Sea, and being pursued by the power of Egypt, and their deliverance by an almighty arm which overturned their enemies; and their being proved by want of bread and water; as also their gross mistake in setting up the Egyptian idol, the golden calf, and dancing before it with this acclamation of joy: "These be thy gods, O Israel." Now I say, all these Ex 32:4 things that happened to Israel in Egypt, through the Red Sea and in the wilderness, have a true resemblance of believers traveling from spiritual Sodom and Egypt, so called. Which is no other than coming from a state of fallen nature in the first Adam, in which all are dead and strangers to God, being in the enmity are chil-

47

dren of wrath, unto a state of grace and life through Jesus Christ, our spiritual Moses, being reconciled to God through him who is the second Adam, the Lord from heaven who never fell. And thus as we are opened by the Spirit, in the ministry of the letter, to hold forth the true meaning of the Spirit, therein we may be instrumental to bring many souls out of the enmity and wrath, to be reconciled to God through Jesus Christ. And this ministry is called the word of reconciliation. "Now then we are ambassadors for Christ, as though God did beseech you by us: we pray you in Christ's stead, be ye reconciled to God." Now I say, a minister ought first to experience the veil that is in the history of the letter, taken away by the operation of Christ's Spirit in his own heart, and the substance of the figures under the law, given to him in experience. This will give him boldness to declare what God has done for his soul, as said the Apostle: "Knowing therefore the terror of the Lord, we persuade men"; that is, we labour to turn men from darkness to light, and from the power of Satan (the spiritual Pharaoh) unto God. And as is before observed, the sense of these terrors may be so acute and sharp upon the spirits of our young preachers, that they may with more charity be excused that warmth of zeal in warning and forewarning others to forsake those evils for which they have so lately and severely smarted. I say, they may be borne with, and charity should be uppermost in our minds towards such, where this is the case.

Now all these aforenamed openings of the Spirit, as we are conducted therein by the Word of Life, are of great use and service in the church to beget faith in unbelievers, to build up and confirm them that have had some taste and feeling of the heavenly gift. And this may so affect some, who have obtained part of the same ministry, that they may be in danger of borrowing one of another, and endeavouring to imitate the same; but not having the same virtue and power attending, the nakedness of such will soon appear. But the danger of borrowing may lie as near, respecting the Scriptures of the Old and New Testament, with any other books that may affect our minds, as what we have heard delivered in the openings of life. For it is no more lawful for us to preach what we have read, because we have read it, than it is for us to preach what we have heard, because we have heard it. Nay, I may further add (what thee will find by experience true in due time) that it is not lawful for thee to repeat thy own experience and former openings, merely in thy own strength of memory and will. For if thee does treasure up and furnish thyself this way, thee will be greatly disappointed, and thy doctrine will be like the manna kept out of season:

Cf.
Ex 16:20
worms bred in it, and it stank. Now a spiritual minister is and ought every day to be like blank paper when he comes into the assembly of the Lord's people, not depending on any former openings or experience, either of his own or others, that he has heard or read. His only and sole dependence must be on the gift of the Spirit, to give and bring to his understanding matter suitable to the present state of the assembly. Thus will thy words be fitly spoken, "like Prv 25:11 apples of gold in pictures of silver," and then thee will appear as the oracle of God, ministering out of that ability which God gives, and under his conduct thee will be safe. Thy words, being full of Spirit and life, will edify the hearers, and thy own heart will be full of comfort and peace, the comfort of the Holy Spirit; which will bring thee great honour and respect from thy brethren, which ought with great care to be received. And the more thee has hereof, the more humble and circumspect ought thee to be in rendering the honour where due, that is, to thy Lord and Master, the Lord Jesus Christ, the great minister and apostle of our profession.

Having brought our young ministers thus far, we will consider them fitted for other services in travelling, which shall be the subject of the next chapter.

CHAPTER V

WE WILL NOW CONSIDER our young minister as having an enlargement of both understanding and love, engaging his mind to labour for the good of others. And this can't be confined to thy own meeting, church, or county, where thee has thy residence; but the constraining power of love, arising from the operation of the gift in thy own mind, may bring thee under a weighty concern to visit the churches abroad, in which work there generally is a gradual beginning; first, in visiting thy neighbouring meetings. And in this work, as thee keeps thy place, thee will gain experience, and thereby come to be more fit to undertake weightier service.

Thus, be not overforward to visit Friends abroad, lest thee should bring thyself under a suspicion of running too fast; neither be too backward, lest thee should hurt thyself by hindering thy growth in that love which would enlarge thy mind for the edifying of the church, and thy own comfort. In order therefore to both, I request a due attention in thy mind, to feel the constraining power of love to draw thy Spirit before thee goes, which will, with a divine affection and ardent desire, move strong in thee for the good of them thee is to visit. Let this rest upon thee, with a resignation that if it be thy place, thee is both ready and willing to go. If these desires arise in thee from a right Spirit, thee will feel great peace in so giving up, with a clear sight and satisfaction in thyself to go. Now after thee has given up to visit thy neighbouring meetings and is come among strange Friends and faces, thee will find thyself under great fears and doubts how thee shall come off. And perhaps it may be poor enough in thy own esteem, so that thee may think thee had better have stayed at home; and a jealousy may possess thy mind, that the Friends judge thee is out of thy place. And thus thee may return under a cloud for thy undertaking, and more especially so if thee finds thyself guilty of slips in expression or doctrine, either in misapplying or misciting the text; this may dull thy spirits, and flag thy inclinations for the present exceedingly. But thee must not rest here, for the gift thee has received will not thus be smothered if thee regards it as thee ought, and the trouble thee meets with may be of good use to thee, which hereafter thee may see (though it does not now appear). Therefore, as thee keeps thy place, thee will find thy heart more ardently inclined to go again, when no doubt thy last visit will be remembered as a block in thy way to so good a work. That ought not hinder, though it will humble thee; but go again, chiefly regarding to look in the proper place for help, where thee has in time past met with it. And if thee comes off well now this second visit, finding all pleased, this may raise thee in thy own thoughts more than may be for thy good, if thee does not watchfully call to mind the foundation of that excellency in which thee has appeared, and give the praise thereof to the Almighty, discouraging in thyself, or any other, anything that may appear contrary thereto. Thus by degrees thee will be more acquainted and inured to strange faces and meetings, and will get strength over that slavish fear and uneasiness, occasioned through want of experience.

As thee witnesses a growth in thy gift, the Word of Life, a concern of greater moment and consequence may fall upon thee. For as thy heart is enlarged in the Word of Life, thy love will be farther extended towards the children of men, and inclinations will be raised in thy mind (in proportion to that love which is begot in thee, by the gift of the Spirit thee has received to minister from) to make farther visits to the meetings and people of God in some adjacent county or counties. Under the impulse whereof thee will find many difficulties and hardships laid in thy way, which will bring thee under a great strait what to do, sometimes concluding this, and sometimes that. While thee is under this doubting, it will be proper to advise with some ministers who have had some experience in the like case, and let them know how it is and has been with thee, respecting thy present concern, and they may be assisting to satisfy thy mind, and thee may from that conclude to give way, being easy and well satisfied it is thy place to go. But before thee takes thy journey, lay the matter before thy brethren, in order for a proper certificate or a letter of recommendation, signifying their satisfaction and unity with thy undertaking. All this being done, the consent of thy friends and brethren obtained, and nothing appearing now to obstruct, give up freely to make this intended visit, always minding that thee keep close to thy gift and follow the leadings thereof both in thy journeyings and doctrine. So will thee find thy strength inwardly to increase, and experience will be daily added to thy knowledge, and thee will be preserved from going too fast in thy travels, or from being persuaded to go out of thy right line and concern; or from lingering too long in particular places, all which are hurtful mistakes when fallen into. But as thy mind is preserved under the conduct of the Spirit and Word of Truth, thee will see when it is thy place to return; and the same constraining power of love in thy heart which drew thee forth, will lead thee home again.

And when thee is there, endeavour to keep thy place in humility, lest thee should miss thy way by endeavouring to appear as an able minister, supposing, because thee has been abroad a little, thee must now give some proof of thy apostleship by enlarging on such matters as come before thee, apprehending that thy friends at home may expect such a performance from thee. If thee should let thy mind out to answer them therein, thee may disappoint thyself as well as those that hear thee. To avoid which, be mindful to regard thy opening, proceeding no farther than led by the Spirit in thy ministry, let it be little or much, without endeavouring to make it more or less. Neither covet to appear well-read or learned; for by giving way to such a temper thee may discover thy weakness, and appear both foolish and impertinent to them that hear thee. It is safe for a minister to desire no other knowledge than the work of regeneration in his own mind, that he may speak to others the things of the Spirit (in such words of plainness as are received from it) because he knows them to be true in his own experience, always remembering that it is not lawful for us to speak our own experience in our own time and will, but we must wait to feel some spiritual virtue and divine assistance in our minds, enabling us, by opening our understandings, to declare to others with power and authority, in the Word of Life, what God has done for our souls. And this will be delivered in such terms and plainness of speech as they that are unlearned and of low capacities will understand. But if we undertake the work in our own time, and depend upon strength of memory, either from what has been opened to us before, or from what we have formerly had in our experience, we shall easily fall under that temptation of endeavouring to appear eloquent, by embellishing our discourse with such terms and phrases as we may not rightly understand, and therefore may misapply. Thus by aspiring to appear knowing, well-read, and eloquent, we may discover our nakedness by aiming at forbidden knowledge, as our first parents did. Our safety therefore stands in keeping to the root of the ministry, the inspiration of the Spirit, patiently waiting at all times to know our places and services in the ministry, that when we speak, it may be the word and mind of the Spirit, and not our own; and when we minister, it may be in the strength and ability which God is pleased to give, and not our own. Thus shall we gain strength, and our labour will be acceptable; the hearts of our brethren will be opened and enlarged towards us, as we thus approve ourselves workmen that rightly divide the Word of Truth. Herein neither we ourselves, nor those that hear us, will have any just cause to be ashamed.

Now as thee thus keeps thy place in thy gift, thee will grow therein, and thy desire and inclinations will likewise with ardent love grow in proportion with thy gift. For the tendency of a spiritual ministry, and its nature, is such that it enflames the mind, wherever it is, with a desire of doing good to the souls of men, and to be instrumental to promote their happiness, both here and hereafter, according to that ability received. And this is no other than the love of God in Christ Jesus, working on thy mind and gently constraining thee to so good a work; and thee will now clearly see that a dispensation of the gospel is given thee in charge, and thy care ought to increase with thy gift, how to discharge thy duty therein. But thee will also find at times very strong reasonings against thy undertaking, nay perhaps stronger than before, and will be ready to think and to say to thyself, "Why should I trouble my mind about these things? I had best mind my own work now I am young, and endeavour to improve myself in the affairs of this life, which will be both prudent and commendable. This I will endeavour, and likewise be as religious and careful of myself as I can, and let others look to themselves for me; that's their duty and not mine." Such like reasonings as these will at times rise very high in thy way. But not-withstanding, as thee keeps to thy gift and waits in it, all these clouds of reasonings will vanish, and thy mind will be secretly enflamed with love to promote faith on the earth.

Now the first journey I supposed very short: soon out and soon home; but presuming the next to be longer, it will be more needful than it was at the first time to have the approbation of the monthly meeting of which thee is a member. And it may so happen that some of thy brethren may think that thee is not qualified for such an undertaking, but they may advise thee to tarry at home till thee is (in their thoughts) better fitted for such a visit. And this may be a very hard trial, which if not rightly taken, may prove hurtful to thy mind. For if thee is apt to be dejected, this may bring thee very low, and stagger thee, so as to call in question the very foundation which thee has thus far proceeded upon in thy ministry; but if thee keeps thy place in thy gift, this will be of great benefit to thee in gaining experience. I say, here will be a great need of keeping a close watch over thy own temper and spirit, lest prejudice should beget hard thoughts in thy mind against those whom thee may look upon as opposers, because they scruple giving consent to thy travelling so long a journey as is proposed. If thee is of a vindictive temper and apt to resent, this may, if thee is not very watchful, tincture thy ministry with bitterness, which will appear by giving slant and side strokes in thy preaching, or by suffering thyself to think that what they offer in opposition to thy travelling proceeds from some private pique or resentment, and not from any just cause of objection that they have to thy ministry, but out of a captious humour they set themselves against thee. And thee to be even with them may give way to passion and resentment, so that thy mind is soured, and thy ministry tinctured with anger and revenge, giving side blows with a view to oppose thy opposers. But whatever thy success may be respecting them, thee may assure thyself, by this conduct thee will expose thyself to contempt with thy best friends, and make thy way more strait, by increasing the number of dissatisfied brethren by thy preaching so full of resentment, and void of gospel love. The more thee strives this way for victory and enlargement, the greater and stronger the opposition will be against thee, and thee will become an object of contempt.

To avoid all the inconveniences that may arise on this account, it will be fit to consider that for every fault or error thee is guilty of in thy travels, whether it be in doctrine or conversation, the meeting and Friends that have recommended thee as a minister must share largely with thee, both in the blame and shame thee brings upon thy profession and ministry by thy ill conduct or disagreeable doctrine. Therefore every Friend in thy own meeting ought to be satisfied, both respecting thy ministry and conduct as a minister, before they sign letters recommendatory on thy behalf. Nay, it is the indispensable duty of every member having a just cause of objection to oppose thy pretensions to travel as a minister, with this caution: that he in a brotherly and gospel spirit show the cause of his objections. And whether it may relate to thy doctrine or conversation, or both, let this mind be in thee: that it is designed for the good of the whole, and with a view to prevent any uneasiness to the Society, and not in any prejudice to thee, but for thine and the church's good. Therefore guard against a spirit of resentment, and keep in love and charity with all those that may appear against thee, desiring above all to be endued with an humble and forgiving spirit. Put the best meaning on what thee has met with, that it was and is designed for thy good, with a view to save both thine and the monthly meeting's credit where thee is a member. Make thy humble application in spirit to God for true wisdom, and the spirit of a sound mind to conduct thee in this time of trial by opposition from such as may wish both thee and the cause of religion right well in general. Keep close to thy gift, forbearing to appear in the ministry if thee feels any tincture of sourness or resentment; but wait in silence until all that is purged out and taken away by the prevailing power of love in Christ Jesus, that so the ministry of reconciliation from him may fill thy mind. And in this, as thee is kept and preserved, thee will through patience overcome all that may oppose thee. Thus will thee, by divine aid, be able to turn thy water (which has been afflicting) into wine, and thy way will be opened, all objections removed, and some whom thee may have looked upon as enemies may appear now thy best friends, who have watched over thee for good. And finding all their objections answered, and uneasinesses concerning thee removed by thy humble, meek, and prudent conduct, they may with both freedom and pleasure consent to sign thy credentials as a minister in unity with them; though they may not all come in at once, but some may receive such impressions, by contesting the point, that it will require time to wear out. But thy strength will increase, and the love of thy brethren grow strong towards thee, for the work's sake.

Thus by faith, having through patience surmounted all these difficulties, thee will find the words of the Apostle true, that "all things work together for good to them that love God." And   Rom 8:28

61

these afflictions and trials will add to thy spiritual improvement, and thee will grow in the root, and thy experience will be much enlarged, and great will be thy comfort and peace. But suppose again that thee meets with no opposition of this kind, but the meeting and every member in it are pleased, and cheerfully recommend thee as a minister in unity with them. Then it is needful to consider that thee has in some good degree the credit and honour of that meeting reposed in thee, of which thee ought for both thy own sake and theirs to be very circumspect and careful, knowing that if thee should bring any disgrace or shame upon thyself, either in thy ministry or conversation, the meeting that has certified on thy behalf will likewise suffer with thee, and come under blame for recommending thee as a minister, finding that thee answers not the character given concerning thee. Under this state thy return will bring both sorrow and shame to thy friends at home. For the avoiding whereof, the next chapter contains some needful cautions and counsel. I conclude this with Paul's advice to Timothy: "I charge thee therefore before God, and the Lord Jesus Christ. . . . Preach the word; be instant in season, out of season; reprove, rebuke, exhort with all longsuffering and doctrine. For the time will come, when they will not endure sound doctrine. . . . But watch thou in all things, endure afflictions, do the work of an evangelist, make full proof of thy ministry." This excellent advice, with that in the close of the second chapter, is worthy of our notice and consideration.

2 Tm 4:1-5

Cf.
2 Tm 2:24-26

CHAPTER VI

CAUTIONS AGAINST PRIDE AND EXALTEDNESS,
MEDDLING IN MATTERS, SPREADING REPORTS, ETC.,
AND A GENERAL RECOMMENDATION
OF HUMILITY AND MEEKNESS
IN ALL THINGS

I NOW SUPPOSE thee ready to take thy journey in unity with thy brethren, manifested by a certificate given thee for that purpose. Thus leaving them in the sweet fellowship of the gospel, having their prayers for thy preservation and success; yet not without great fear, and it may be weeping thee sets out, doubting how it may answer. Thee may perhaps be well satisfied for a few meetings at thy first setting out in this great humility of mind; but thee must then keep so humble and inward with the Lord in spirit, as to wait daily for the renewings of both wisdom and power from him. Thus will thy mind be supplied, every meeting, with new life and matter suiting the states of the people thee is among; and this will be to thy comfort and peace, and to their edification.

But if after these fresh supplies that thee daily is favoured with, thee should grow unmindful what thee really is, and begin to think thyself in a better capacity for the work than formerly, and the esteem and favour shown thee by thy friends begins to swell thy mind above that humble and depending frame; thee will find after such a state of mind prevails upon thee that leanness and barrenness of soul will ensue. And if thee does not bethink thyself seasonable to return, but endeavours in thy own strength and will to save thy credit as a minister, thee will lose ground faster than it was gained. Thus some, after they have begun well, and gone on so for some time, having gained some experience and a form of sound words, but for want of keeping humble and inward in spirit with the Lord, they have insensibly gone from the foundation and spring of living ministry, and depended on memory, former experience, and openings, and not on the inspiration of the Spirit, which is the root of all true ministry, and what proceeds from it always new and acceptable. I say, such have fallen into repetitions of the same things, without a newness of virtue attending them therein, and so have become formal ministers in the oldness of the letter.

And this sort of preaching may take with some, especially those that are unsensible of the virtue of the Spirit to reveal unto them the things of the Spirit of God. But notwithstanding thee may have favour and credit with such as a preacher, and may be by those respected for a little time, and regarded as such; yet the longer that thee goes on in this way, the more thee will covet honour and preeminence, yea, thee will in time be apt to seek the praise of men more than of God, and out of humour, being displeased if thee has it not. But alas, this is poor work; for by the living in religion thee will soon be discovered, and found out to be but an empty, dry, and unfruitful formalist. They that are alive unto God will see thee plainly to be such; for the Lord's people, who have a spiritual discerning, can't be long imposed upon, but they will find out, and discover the true voice from the false, loving the first, and thee for the sake thereof; but rejecting the last, and the authors thereof, be they whoever they may. Therefore all thy contrivance, forecast, and skill, used to the utmost advantage in thy own time, will, and strength, will prove but as a broken cistern that can hold no water that will ever afford refreshment to the people of God, but will load and grieve them.

To avoid all which, it will be safe to keep in an humble dependence, endeavouring to keep near the Lord, having him always before our eyes, that we may receive daily ability from him, and speak as we feel our minds moved by his divine Spirit. And whether it be little or much that we have to say, be thankful that we are favoured with his presence and life in our ministry, not so much regarding what others may say or judge concerning us, as the peace and satisfaction that we inwardly enjoy by the Word of Life, that life which is the light of men. Thee may find thyself as this day drawn forth and greatly enlarged in thy ministry, but tomorrow thee may be shut up, barren and poor, having but very little to say, and that but very brokenly, as with a stammering tongue, which may seem very uneasy to thee so to appear; and under such a condition thee may be tempted to go beyond thy commission. This ought always to be watched against, for it is our safest and best way, at all times, to appear just as we feel power and strength in our gifts, endeavouring to keep our minds in patience, be it how it will, knowing that the wind blows where, when, as strong, and weak, as it listeth, and we can neither add nor diminish ought from it. But if in the time of weakness we endeavour to hide ourselves by multiplying words, we shall discover still more weakness, and in this state silence will be much more safe than preaching. Therefore if thee has but little to say, say little; and if thee has nothing to say, be silent. For although thee may be judged as out of thy place in travelling, having nothing to preach, yet if any count this as a fault to be ashamed of, it is to be considered that this re-puted shame (for in reality it is thy credit) will

Cf.
Jn 3:8

67

fall more directly upon thyself in thy undertaking to preach without any authority for so doing. For by such an undertaking thee may fall unawares into such impertinences that may be a real shame, both to thyself and thy brethren also, who will hereby share deeply with thee, and the principle be reproached for thy folly and forwardness in pretending to inspiration when thee has it not. Therefore, if at times thee is very poor and has nothing to say, let not this tempt thee to go beyond thy line; for this poverty and affliction thee is under may by divine purpose be brought upon thee, to prepare thy mind to speak more feelingly and with moving language to others under the like distress and barrenness of soul. Thus are the ministers of Christ often, as it may be said, baptized for the dead, that is, they are given to taste of the various and near trials that believers are exercised and proved by, and are likewise made to taste and feel of the infinite mercy of God in raising them from death to life, and from the power of Satan and darkness, to partake of the joys of immortality and eternal life, brought to light again by the gospel.

And when a minister is thus prepared by spiritual affliction, occasioned by the withdrawing of divine virtue from his mind, and suffered, as many good persons have been, to be buffeted, tempted, tried, and sifted by Satan, feeling faith, hope, and patience almost to fail; yet in this state, by a secret and hidden power, neither seen nor thought of, he is preserved; though for very anguish he may be ready to cry out in the bitterness of his soul, "Oh! wretched man that I am, to undertake what I was not called to, and to run before I was sent. My punishment is greater than I can bear." Thus it pleases God to suffer his ministers to be proved, that they may come forth as vessels fit for the refiner.

But then, when this Deliverer is pleased to reveal himself the beloved of the souls, oh! what exceeding joy, what exceeding soul satisfaction then! Oh! then a minister can from experience cry out and say, "Come taste and see that God is good, and worthy to be waited upon. Oh! come, and I'll tell you what God has done for my soul."

Now this ministry begets faith, and raises the hearers' minds up unto the lively hope of the gospel, the power of life, in the preaching of the Word as the oracles of God, and in that ability we receive from him.

Here we find such kind of trials and afflictions by poverty and barrenness to turn both to ours and the church's good, as we keep the Word of God's patience. And though in this state of poverty and weakness, sympathizing friends are very few, and such as will frown and look strange upon us may be many; yet nevertheless, such whose eyes are upon us, some for evil and some for good, will see that our excellency is in him that has called us to this work, and not in ourselves. And in due time, as we keep in humility and patience, waiting in our gifts, we shall be drawn forth and enlarged to the satisfaction of them that hear us. The scale may come to be turned, and thee may now have more to admire and speak in thy praise than thee had to frown upon thee. For such is the fickleness and uncertainty of many in this respect, that they will turn both with us and against us in a short time, so that the more applause we have, the more fearful of ourselves we ought to be. But if we should be exalted in ourselves, by reason that we are admired by common fame, we may, before we are aware of it, bring ourselves into the same condition before described, and all that friendship may be turned into slight and enmity again. It is therefore very safe for us at all times to keep humble and inward with the Lord, waiting in our gifts, that we may truly know when to speak and what, as likewise when to be silent. Herein we shall grow from one degree of experience to another, the gospel will be purely preached, and the work will prosper in our hands.

Next, be careful of thy conversation; for it may so happen that where thee lodges, either casually or designedly thee may hear of some difference subsisting among Friends, and others may likewise expose some vices that some of their meeting may be addicted to, of which they will be pleased thee take notice. To all such kind of discourses thee ought to give no heed, but rather with decency shun them, lest they should bias thy mind in thy ministry, and so thee may preach by information more than by inspiration; this will hurt thy service and reputation. But if after thy service is over, thee meets with anything of this kind, and can have freedom to advise, or be serviceable in any respect to set right things which are amiss, endeavour to keep in the way of thy duty with all humility and patience, considering impartially what is said on all sides. Then meekly persuade to peace rather than judge among them, for it may be dangerous to judge on either side without a fair hearing, lest thee should give strength to that which thee ought not; but if we can in a friendly manner bring contending parties to an agreement, we shall do a good work. And if we have any advice to give to the disorderly and vicious, let it be done in much love and tenderness, rather showing the evil consequences of such practices by comparison in other men (which may show them their folly) than to fall directly upon them. By this way of reproof, Nathan brought David to pass sentence upon himself; and if thee is instrumental to set their folly in a clear light, they may thereby be prevailed on to reform and amend. Thy prudent conduct herein will much increase both thy service and peace.

Next, be careful not to carry tales and reports from one place to another; for some have, by such work, made themselves very offensive; and consider that talebearing is forbidden under Cf. Lv 19:16 the law, as of pernicious consequence to the peace of society. How base then must it appear in a gospel minister, to be guilty of this folly? Therefore, if thee is at any time informed of ought concerning any Friend that may injure his character, first enquire whether such an informer has given such a one gospel order;* and whether, if he be called upon to vouch what he has said, he will abide by that report? This will be a means to put a stop to talebearing in a good degree. Yet for all this, if thee finds a concern to advise with such a one, and to let him know what thee has heard concerning his or her conduct, minding that prohibition Cf. Ex 23:1 against false reports, this will make it needful,

*"Gospel order" as here used refers to the steps recommended in Matt. 18:15-17 when one Christian disagrees with another. Quakers also use the term to refer to the way in which the Holy Spirit organizes ("orders") the individual and corporate lives of a group fully surrendered to the work of Christ in its midst.

if what thee has heard be questioned as to its truth, for thee to make known thy authors, to make out what they have reported. And if it appears on examination false, a stop will be put to it, which otherwise, by the method of "I will tell thee but do thee keep it to thyself" might go far and wide. This conduct will be as a fortress against all such busy people, who love to scan their neighbours' failings while they overlook their own; and thy credit will grow with thy friends, and thy gift will make room for thee, as thee is thus preserved. But if thee should have a pleasure in and encourage such tattling, thee will hurt thy service, and feed that temper in others as well as in thyself which ought to be slain. Therefore, never hear nor receive any such report but from such judicious Friends who have laboured in a spirit of love to reclaim such offenders, and want thy aid to strengthen their endeavours already used for the good of such; which is what in justice, according to gospel doctrine, we owe one to another. This kind of behaviour will answer thy character, and thee will have praise for the same.

In the course of thy travels thee will have frequent opportunities with Friends at their meetings of discipline, wherein there may happen sometimes warm debates, which may, if thee is not very careful and reserved, be a snare to thee in thy conduct; and thee may be too easily provoked to speak on one side or the other before thee rightly knows and understands the matter. Now, although I would have us be very careful and cautious how we meddle at such times and in such meetings, yet I would that we should exercise both our ears and understandings, waiting in our gifts; perhaps we may have a service in reconciling matters in debate. And if thee finds it thy place to speak, be upon the enquiry, to find yet more clearly the right thing that is contended for, and let thy words be delivered with great deference and regard to both parties, with that decent condescension, submission, and sweetness that is becoming thy age and experience to treat thy friends with.

If thee should likewise observe a difference in the management of their affairs, respecting their discipline in common, from what it is in the meeting whereof thee is a member, and from this may judge thyself able to show them a better method, which method by custom is become familiar to thee, and if thee is forward to dictate, by endeavouring to persuade them to alter their method of ordering matters, thee may be looked upon as a busy meddler in what concerns thee not. But if in private conversation some better notions of management respecting the making such meetings more serviceable, to answer the good end proposed by them for the benefit of the Society, can be cultivated in the minds of those concerned, and so propagated by degrees, it might be of great use. But hasty revolutions and changes in forms of discipline are of dangerous consequence, and ought never to be attempted but upon considerations well digested. For it may offend some and unsettle others by raising debates for and against, which may cause great heats if they be stiff on both sides, as it may likely so fall out, to the breach of unity, and lessening brotherly love and charity one towards another.

I have observed, that where a monthly or quarterly meeting have continued in the method recommended to them by some worthy elders who are now gone, and left this practice as it were a legacy to them, some have been very much opinionated thereof, in honour to the founders of the method they may be in. We, not knowing the reason inducing such worthy elders to this or that way of management, ought to be very tender in judging about things of this nature. It may not be so material whether things may be done this or that way for the good of the whole, so they be done in charity and love. Therefore let us in our travels take care not hastily to meddle and dip into these affairs, and so do more hurt than good.

Now as to thy private conduct in all places where thee is with thy friends: be very modest and thankful for such entertainment as may be given thee. Though it may be but (in thy esteem) poor and mean, yet as thee has it from a sincere, loving, hearty and honest mind, according to the ability of the giver, be content, thankful and cheerful with it; remembering who said, "He that gives a cup of cold water to a prophet, in the name of a prophet, shall have a prophet's reward." And guard against speaking disrespectfully in any other place of that entertainment (though mean), for that may be very offensive, and give great uneasiness, being a hurt to thyself more than thee may be aware of; but in these matters behave as becomes thy place and service.

Cf.
Mt 10:41-42

And in thy conversation, whether in public, or more privately with those of a different sex, be strictly careful to avoid too great familiarities, and everything which, though innocent in itself, may give any just occasion of offence to such who may be watching over thy conduct, either with a good or evil eye; that so thee may not only be preserved from evil, but likewise from every appearance thereof. By a prudent and inoffensive behaviour adorn the gospel of God our Saviour, and be an example to the believers, not only in word and doctrine in public, but likewise in private, in conversation, in charity, in spirit, in faith, and in purity.

And if thee is unmarried, carefully guard against either making or receiving any proposals to alter thy condition hastily, and without being well advised, and seeing thy way clear therein. Finish thy journey first, let the other rest till that is over; so will thee avoid the risk of any reproach that might fall upon thee for any misbehaviour in that matter.

Take what care thee can, according to thy ability, not to make the gospel chargeable to thy friends in going from one place to another; neither be difficult to please in such places, but always show thyself easy and contented with such entertainment as can be had. Some tempers, though strait handed enough themselves, are yet difficult to please, and apt to find fault, giving by such conduct uneasiness to their friends. But as we have no views of reward from our hearers, we ought not to desire any other than a little supply for the present occasion of what is needful to eat and drink, for which let us be thankfully contented, and not show any uneasiness if what is set before us doesn't so well suit our present wants; but consider the ability of the Friends where we are, who may exceed their common way of living considerably, the better to accommodate us. A discontented and murmuring spirit has done hurt, and given occasion for some to say that the design of such in going abroad was to eat and drink, more than to preach the gospel. A reflection I hope every Friend in his travel will take care to avoid, and take all occasions to prevent; not forgetting that all the malice the world and the devil have vented against the true ministry among us could never fix the odium upon us justly of being mercenary, that is, such who ever looked for gifts or sought after rewards: a leprosy affecting all the hireling teachers in the world, of what kind soever.

Dear brethren, let us maintain in our conduct that noble way we have ever walked in: that as we have freely received our ministry from God by his Spirit, freely to give to the people. For a free ministry will stand, and be continued in the church to latest posterity; but the hirelings will be rejected more and more, and come to nought by degrees.

Next, where thee comes, enquire if there are any sick, either in body or mind, among them, and wait to know thy place and freedom in thy gift to visit such. But in all such visits, let thy words be few and weighty, for if thee should give way thyself to much discourse, or indulge it in those thee visits, it may hurt thy service to them, and render it void. Therefore regard

78

the weight of thy gift to open thy understanding, that whether thee may be opened in some short exhortations, or by way of prayer, what thee has may be from thy gift, not then doubting but thee may be instrumental of good to them thee so visits. But some apprehend that when they are with the sick, in either body or mind, they must be preaching, praying, or discoursing, perhaps beyond due bounds, which sometimes have proved rather a burden and grief to the afflicted than a comfort.

And if thee observes in any a slackness or an undue liberty taken, not so agreeable to their profession, unto whom thee finds thy mind engaged to speak by way of advise or caution, let it be done in the spirit of meekness and love, that if possible, thee may reach the witness in their minds that what thee says is right. Thus having discharged thy duty as a minister, both in a public and private capacity, that is, in the assemblies and private families where thy lot has fallen, thee will return with great joy and consolation, finding the words of the royal prophet fulfilled: "He that goeth forth and weepeth, bearing precious seed, shall doubtless come again with rejoicing, bringing his sheaves with him." Ps 126:6

CHAPTER VII

ADVICE TO MINISTERS IN THE STATE OF YOUNG
MEN, WHEREIN SELF-CONCEIT OF THEMSELVES,
AND TOO LOW ESTIMATION OF OTHERS, MAY BE
APT TO RAISE THE MIND ABOVE THE LOW AND
HUMBLE STATE WHEREIN ITS SAFETY ONLY IS

I SHALL NOW CONSIDER our young minister as grown to a considerable degree of knowledge and experience in the work, and in part to the state of a young man that is strong, in whom the Word dwells more plentifully. Thy reputation as a minister growing with thy gift, thee may now be looked upon in thy own meeting as a member of some weight, to whom thy brethren pay a considerable regard; in which state new trials and temptations may arise, and thee may be in as much danger (in sundry particulars) if not more, to miss thy way, than when less looked upon, both by thyself and others. Now thy friends may apply to thee for advice and counsel under their difficulties, and if thee should happen to mistake, and advise wrong, thee will be blamed, and the hurt sustained by following thy counsel will be laid upon thee as an excuse to themselves thus: "If such a one had not advised me to it, I should not have done it," and this may bring some uneasiness upon thee, very hard to bear without resentment, and endeavouring to vindicate thy advice given as suitable at that time, laying the blame (if any) on the mismanagement of the person advised. Sometimes a small spark of contention thus kindled has risen to a flame. To avoid which, be very cautious in giving advice in difficult cases without very good grounds for what thee says, and advise the parties to consult those of greater experience and judgment, to excuse thy meddling therein. So will thee be free from blame on all hands. Yet I would not have thee peremptorily to refuse hearing the complaints of persons under trouble, that may really want advice and help; but when thee has heard, consider if their trouble arises from any misunderstanding on any account, and whether some way can't be found out for their relief by mediation and persuasion of persons not concerned in the matters under dispute. Thus may thee be instrumental in making peace without dipping into the matter, which is the chief cause of complaint, and this will add to thy credit as a useful member of the body.

Next, thee may now appear with more boldness in thy ministry, which if not duly tempered with modesty, humility, wisdom and meekness, may render thee unpleasant to the ears of them that hear thee, and more especially if thy doctrine should favour more of the man than it did in time past, when thee appeared in the innocency and infancy of the ministry. And this conduct may raise up sundry of the meeting to watch over thee, with a view to have something to lay hold of to thy prejudice, yet intending (at least pretending) thy good, to instruct thee better, and humble thee. Then if thee mistakes or misapplies any Scripture, or drops anything that may not seem safe to be stood by in thy preaching, it may be handed about (if thee is high and uneasy at reproof) from one to another privately, until it comes to thy knowledge, and thee may then find it hard to live under it (more especially) if thee is of a vindictive and high spirit, not able to bear contradiction and reproof, as becomes a minister of Christ. It will therefore be prudent to consider thy natural temper and disposition of mind, endeavouring to keep thyself under subjection to the mortifying power of the cross, that thy doctrine may be adorned with meekness, and also seasoned with gospel salt. In this state judicious Friends will love and vindicate thy service. But if thee gives way to thy own spirit, and in the heat thereof attempts to minister, and vindicate thyself over the heads of thy offended friends, this will render thy doctrine unpleasant to the ear, and bring thee under more disgrace. Finding thyself under a slight, and in some degree of contempt with and among thy brethren, take care that thee does not unawares (in the heat and height of thy own spirit, which is not able to bear evil report) begin to chide, and think to threaten them into a better temper by blaming their conduct in thy preaching as directly as the case will bear. Assure thyself that this conduct and behaviour will be a direct way to turn all their hearts against thee as one man. Thus, instead of gaining on them, and removing the cause of offence, it will be more established, and grow much more difficult to remove for the future, being thus fixed by thy imprudent conduct. Some I have in my time known, from so small a beginning as is before described, to grow (in bitterness and envy, occasioned by spiritual pride and self-conceit) to such a head, as have in time rendered them (who in their beginning were esteemed as ministers) altogether useless, and they have degenerated by degrees so far as to become enemies to the Society, and have left it under great prejudices, in bitterness doing all their degenerate minds might dictate to render the Society contemptible, and its principles odious; which is a dreadful thing to happen to anyone that has ever had a part of this divine ministry.

It is therefore highly needful for us to learn to *know ourselves,* and to keep in it daily, and not to forget and lose the sense of the imperfections and defects in the natural constitution of our own minds. If we find ourselves of an imperious, insulting, proud temper by nature, uneasy at affronts, and not able to endure evil reports without using endeavours to vindicate our honour at all events, not considering what our great Master suffered for us to bring us to the knowledge of himself; let us mind that "Pride goeth before destruction, and an haughty *(unforgiving)* spirit before a fall." I say, if we by nature are so inclined as above, how carefully ought we to keep a watch against that weak part we see in ourselves, praying with sincerity that our minds may be daily improved by a divine cultivation through the Spirit, that that great change may be known upon us, spoken of by the prophet Isaiah: "The wolf also shall dwell with the lamb, and the leopard shall lie down with the kid; and the calf and the young lion and the fatling together; and a little child shall lead them." This is that disposition and subjection of mind that we ought to wait daily to be kept under by the Spirit. If we by nature are like the wolf, leopard, or lion at any time, and that nature appears in us, this by the meek Spirit of Jesus ought to be always kept under subjection and government. For though we may have known our natural tempers subdued in a great degree, at our first setting out in the ministry, by the cross and power of Christ, yet if there be not a daily abiding under that power, our natural inclinations and tempers

84

may prevail again to our hurt, and the blessed effect of that subjection to the Spirit, spoken of by the Prophet, we shall not experience, that is: "They shall not hurt nor destroy in all my holy mountain: for the earth shall be full of the knowledge of the Lord, as the waters cover the sea." Is 11:9

It is therefore needful to watch daily against everything in ourselves that will hurt our service and render our ministry unprofitable, by letting in any resentment or heart-burning against any Friend for a real or supposed affront that may have been put upon us by them; considering that nothing can hurt us that is either said or reported, though with ever so ill a design against us, if we are in our places, and innocent of the things reported. I say, such things can't be hurtful to us, unless we make them so to ourselves by undue resentment, being influenced thereby to preach and entertain an assembly with our private resentment, endeavouring to revenge this supposed injustice done us in this public manner; not considering the force of our Saviour's caution in this case: "Therefore if thou bring thy gift to the altar, and there rememberest that thy brother hath ought against thee; leave there thy gift before the altar, and go thy way; first be reconciled to thy brother, and then come and offer thy gift." The sum of which to our purpose is Mt 5:23-24

85

this: that we undertake not the work of the ministry under the influence of any resentment or private pique in our minds against any brother, but that the sole motive and influence of our ministry ought to be our love to God and the souls of men; and by divine inspiration to labour therein with diligence and sincerity to promote faith in the earth, by stirring up their minds to live a pious and godly life. And as our standing and labour is in this love, we need not fear but our service will be both honourable and acceptable where we live. In this temper of mind we shall be capable to receive instruction (and not think ourselves above it, which is a very dangerous state) and if reproof should be given us in a wrong mind, we being in a right one, may reap good by what is not so intended for us. In this temper of mind we shall see our water turned into wine, and all our bitters made sweet to us; and as before observed, all things will work together for our good, because our standing is in the love and fear of God, and in it we labour by inspiration, as ambassadors of Christ, to make full proof of our ministry for the convincing of gain-sayers, that they may be reconciled unto God, and to build up the believers in that most holy faith, the fruit whereof is righteousness and godly living.

But if thee is of a meek, modest, and bashful

temper, that is, backward, not willing to put thyself forward, but by a mean and low esteem that thee entertains of thy own gift and service, thee puts more value on everybody's performance than thy own, this will (if not tempered with a degree of ardency to do thy day's work in the daytime) do thee much hurt, and very much hinder thy improvement and growth in thy gift. For which reason it is really needful to have a good value for the gift received (mark for the gift, not for ourselves). But then this good liking that we have of our gifts and services ought to be tempered with judgment and modesty; otherwise it may lead to self-conceit and imprudence, which are bad ingredients in the minds of preachers, and will be apt to render them both contemptible and troublesome in their conduct.

But some are always repining, and thinking meanly of their gifts and services, which is a wrong mind; and where it prevails will do hurt, and hinder our improvement and growth. We ought to consider that every gift of God is good, and ought to be regarded as such. He or she that has the smallest and least degree of a gift in the ministry, as they wait in it, and mind to keep to it, and neither on the one hand go before it, nor on the other neglect it, but carefully mind the openings of it and follow its leadings, they will in due time by experience find an enlargement both of matter and spiritual understanding, which will give them great encouragement to go on. I have known sundry such become able ministers, and of very great service in the church; and I have known others, as well as myself, that have begun very poor, and seemed contemptible and mean in the eyes of their friends, nay, have been advised to desist, as not being called to that work, nor qualified for such service, which is very wounding and discouraging. In which time some kind sympathizing Aquilla or Priscilla have been concerned to heal the wound, by instructing more perfectly in the way of the ministry, by giving proper advice and encouragement to go on in the work under the government of the divine Spirit, with a meek and humble conduct; advising on the one hand not to take too much notice of what others may say in dispraise of thy service, but endeavouring to remove their objections by a prudent behaviour; nor on the other, too much regarding what may be said in commendation thereof. For without exercising judgment, the former may cast down too much, and the latter may exalt the mind above its place.

How safe therefore is it to keep in our gifts, under the power and influence of divine love, which will take all things in good part, whether it be praise or dispraise, and not be moved by either out of our place. Thus will malice be overcome by love, and we shall receive advantage even from them that intend us none; being likewise guarded against that poison which flattery and commendation carries with it to weak minds, for some can't bear to be commended, even when they deserve it, without receiving hurt by it, taking that honour to themselves which is only due to their gifts. And being disgusted if they have not commendation and praise, supposing themselves injured without it, rather than not have it, they will seem by a kind of enquiry to beg it, and endeavour, by either finding fault with or commending their service, to draw praise from others. Whoever fall into this practice show great weakness; and it is a plain indication that such are not in the simplicity of the gospel. For whoever abide in that seek not themselves nor their own honour; but the chief thing they have in view is the honour of God and the good of all men, that their ministry may bring honour to him that has called us to glory and virtue.

There are yet some things further to be remarked, relating to our conduct in our own families, meetings, and neighbourhood, both in a religious and civil capacity, which shall be the subject of the next chapter.

CHAPTER VIII

MISCELLANEOUS ADVICES AS TO MARRIAGE,
TRADE, AND AN UNBLAMABLE CONDUCT

WE WILL CONSIDER our minister now as one inclining to marriage, and to settle and have a family, with business and trade in the world; in which state of life there are many dangers and snares which we ought to guard against, and carefully mind our conduct therein. That I may be the more intelligible, I shall treat advices on the whole under these four heads following:

- Respecting thy courtship and marriage, if yet unmarried.

- Thy conduct in thy own family.

- Thy conduct among thy neighbours in trade, commerce, etc.

- Thy conduct in thy own meeting, both as a minister and elder.

In thy courtship or being courted, well consider the object of thy affections. Let not thy mind out after what he or she has, but rather regard what they are, and how qualified both in nature and religion: a good natural temper in both sexes being much preferable to wealth, and more especially when it is cultivated and made better by religion.

Now this being a matter of great consequence requires a serious thought and close examination in our own minds, that we may not be deceived by any false gloss, report or appearance; but thee should narrowly examine the moving cause of thy inclinations, that so thee may with safety and caution begin thy suit, or accept such an offer if a woman. Thus, when thy mind is fixed, and thee is resolved to proceed, begin where thee ought, and be a good example, by first advising with such as may be thy true and hearty friends, before thee makes any offer, or receives one, so as to join in with any proposal on that account. And if they agree with thee, this will add to thy satisfaction; but if by reasons and good arguments they endeavour to dissuade thee, be not above advice in this (or any other affair), but give ear to good counsel. If no objection arises, then apply thyself for consent to parents or guardians before any proposal is made to the object of thy choice; having thus paved thy way, thy work will be much easier afterward. Then proceed deliberately, that thee may give no just cause of offence in thy conduct, but that thy marriage may be completed with a good reputation both to thy own and Friends' satisfaction, and this will add to thy credit as a minister. But when this is over and thee is married, thee must expect new exercises, under which thy faith and patience may be closely proved.

Therefore look well to thy conduct in thy own family, that thee may keep all things sweet and honourable therein. Many are the temptations we are in danger to receive hurt by, such as aspiring too high in our living, aiming to have all other matters suiting thereto, that is, our furniture for our houses, clothes, etc., which if above our ability to support will bring upon us a train of inconveniences, not easily to be surmounted. And such who are of low circumstances, who have travelled in the ministry or may travel, seeing so many various ways of living, may receive hurt if they do not carefully consider their own circumstances and ability. Such should not mind high things, but being subject to their own low estate, should content themselves to live and appear according as they can afford, not endeavouring to live above their ability, so that they will come as near in imitation as they can to such who are above them. Rather let our income be the rule and government of our expenses in living; for if our expense go beyond our income, we shall soon be hurt; but if within, we are safe. And although this parsimonious way of living may, by such as know not our estate, be blamed, and we may be esteemed too near and close, yet as we take care to keep a conscience justly void of offence both towards God and men, we are safe so far. And those who are favoured with better circumstances in this world should not live in pride and exaltation, but walk in humility and godly fear, and let their moderation in eating and drinking, in furniture and apparel, and in all other respects be known unto all men; and what superfluity they have above what may be sufficient for themselves and families, to bestow in doing good to all, but especially to the household of faith. By thus using the blessings of providence, they will be as lights in the world, or as a city set upon a hill, which cannot be hid, but will shine forth to the praise of our great Master, and they at last be entitled to the blessed sentence or invitation of those who have fed the hungry, clothed the naked, and visited the prisoner, which is: Enter into the joy of thy Lord, to dwell in his presence forever.

Cf.
Mt 25:34-36

Next, if thee has children, endeavour to train them up in the nurture and admonition of the Lord, and in a plain, exemplary dress, discouraging them in everything, both in their dress and discourse, that appears inconsistent with that plainness which a minister's children ought to appear in, that they may be exemplary to others. Endeavour early to inculcate in their minds such principles of religion and truth as frequently are held forth in the Holy Scriptures, which as soon as they are capable to read, accustom them to, and endeavour to make them take pleasure therein by explaining such portions thereof as may suit their capacities, that as they advance in age, they may in knowledge; this is the method to "train up a child in the way that he should go." But education, though with the strictest care and tenderness administered, will not answer what some expect from it as to the grounding of youth in true religion and saving faith; for nothing short of the work of grace in the heart, the new birth, and the washing of regeneration by the Word can make a sound and right Christian, and a true minister. We do not come to these attainments by a natural inheritance of birthright from our parents, but by a spiritual relation; for we must be born again before we can see the kingdom of God. And the explaining and opening these divine truths to them, as they are capable to receive and understand the same, will be the best part of their education, and may stand for a witness of our care against their folly when we are gone; for which cause it behooves us that we encourage in them every appearance of virtue, and discourage every vice which human nature is liable to. And be a good example both to thy family, and others also, in diligently attend-

Prv 22:6

94

ing religious meetings with as many of them as thee can with conveniency take with thee; thus will thee be exemplary to the rest of the meeting.

It may be thy lot to be exposed to sufferings for the testimony of a good conscience, which thee ought to be very careful to maintain for thy own peace, standing faithful therein, not at all doubting that a blessing will attend thee, if thee is upright. And if thee is imprisoned for the same, this may prove a close trial both to thee and thy wife; and for this reason, if she is uneasy, and has not faith and courage to stand such a shock, give her all the encouragement thee is capable of, lest through weakness she be prevailed upon, by any indirect compliance with thy adversary, to make the matter up, which will be a hurt to thy ministry and an evil example to thy brethren; both which ought with a prudent and due care to be guarded against.

Add to this thy charitable disposition in contributing to the poor, and other public services in the Society, with thy brethren; in which thee ought to be as good an example as thy ability will admit, being rather above than under, endeavouring to save it another way in thy expenses. For although we encourage charity and a public spirit by words to others, yet if we do not confirm them by our example, they will be of little force. And though I have recommended a close and parsimonious way of living, prudently conducted, yet I would have thee, in thy administerings to the poor, appear generous and noble, thy ability considered; and this will add authority to thy gift.

But perhaps the world may frown upon thee, and thee may find things run cross. This may much hinder thy generosity in charity, and by this thy mind may be much distressed; and unless thee is very careful in keeping thy heart close to thy gift, being inward with the Lord, praying that thy faith and patience fail not, thee will meet with some discouragement. But if thee remains faithful, thee will find this will prepare and fit thy mind to speak more feelingly to others in the like state; although it is very hard to behave under such trials as becomes a minister without a close attending on our gifts in meekness and fear. Let us therefore consider that such trials are by the kindness of providence sometimes suffered to come upon us for our good, to prepare us to speak to others with a better effect, and to prove our faith and patience, as it is written: "Behold, I have refined thee, but not with silver; I have chosen thee in Is 48:10 the furnace of affliction." This distress may wear off, and things in a short time may assume another face. Then beware of being exalted;

for as affliction and poverty, without faith and patience, can't be borne without receiving hurt; so prosperity, without humility in a steady attention upon God in our gifts, will have the like effect upon us. This brings me to the third head, relating to thy conduct among thy neighbors in trade and commerce.

Trade is sometimes very dangerous, and apt to deceive the mind, by influencing it with hopes of more gain to launch out beyond our strength and capacity. I therefore have ever found it most safe to bound my extent in trade by my stock, and as that increased, the other might with much more safety. Thus I carefully avoided going beyond my strength, which would render it impossible for me to keep my word and promise in payments; for I saw this brought me under such a necessity that I could not buy, neither sell so well, but sometimes must raise money (by selling at a low rate, under the market) or else hurt my credit in payments. I therefore took this method: whensoever I contracted for a parcel of goods, first to consider what pay I could make before I made an agreement, and then bought as cheap as I could, for such credit as we could agree upon; and when it so happened (as sometimes it did) that without borrowing I could not pay as I promised (which is the life of trade), then a little before the day came, I went and told

my dealer how it was with me; yet nevertheless, if necessity called for the money, I would
provide it by the time, but hoping by such a
day I could make payment of my own strength,
if he could stay so long. By this conduct, I
found a readiness in all my dealers to favour
me as desired, if no great necessity did prevent
it. Thus by degrees I increased both my stock
and trade, proceeding in it both with repute
and honour. And on this account I became
more taken notice of, and my company by
some more desired, which I soon found would
grow upon me to my hurt, if a stop were not
put to it. Above all, I found it very dangerous
to meddle with strong liquors of any kind but
in a very moderate way, especially drams,
which have been very hurtful to the health of
several. I thus endeavoured to steer my course
as inoffensively as I could in trade and commerce, by keeping my word and promise in
payments, which added much to my credit.

Lastly, in thy own meeting be a good example
to attend in season, at the hour appointed, both
on first and week days, with as many of thy
family as can be spared. And when there, do
not attempt either to preach or pray without
some degree of divine love, begot by the Spirit,
to inspire thee to it; for by the Word of Life
we must be qualified before we can either
preach or pray to advantage. Some think,

through a mistaken judgment, that they must be doing something every meeting (like the preachers of the letter, who must either be singing, preaching or praying all the time), and by such a conduct they lose their interest and place in the hearts of Friends by too long and too frequent appearing in both preaching and prayer. For the avoiding of which, keep close to thy gift, intently waiting to know thy place, both when to speak and when to be silent. And when thee speaks begin under a sense of divine influence, whether it be in preaching or praying; without it, do not either preach or pray; for silent meetings, though a wonder to the carnal and worldly professors, are of great advantage to the truly spiritually minded. And as thee begins with the Spirit, keep to it in thy going on, and conclude in it, and this will preserve thee from tiring thy brethren, and causing them to wish for thy silence. Thus as thee begins and goes on in the openings of divine life, thy service as a minister in thy own meeting will be always new and living. Thus will thee engage the attention of thy hearers to what thee has to declare, all which will tend to the improvement of thyself and edification of thy brethren.

Add to this a prudent conduct in meetings of business or discipline, and watch against thy own spirit and temper, and by no means let them arise under colour of zeal for the cause, that thee may not lust after power and rule. In some, such a mind prevails that they are not easy without they can rule and overrule their brethren. But if thee keeps thy place in thy gift, thee will take thy friends along with thee, that you may go hand in hand in the work, carefully guarding against all selfish and private views, from resentment taken against a brother or sister for any supposed offence, either against thyself or any of thy friends. The falling into any little mistake of this kind will have a train of other inconveniences to attend it, such as making parties, and falling into divisions, one party against another, and opposing one the other, to the great hurt of the Society. Let us with diligence watch against and discourage, both in ourselves and also among the brethren, every appearance of both party taking and party making, and in all our views and endeavours sincerely labour to promote unity and peace. For it rarely happens, when such ruptures fall out in monthly or quarterly meetings, but the strong and zealous sticklers on either side receive much hurt by taking offence, which in a more particular manner hurts ministers and makes their work much more difficult, if it does not wholly lay waste and set their service aside; therefore they, in an especial manner, ought to be mediators, by endeavouring to bring both parties to an agreement if possible.

But I do not mean by this that the authority of the discipline should be broke in upon by unruly and disorderly spirits, who are unwilling to submit to the rules and wholesome doctrines of the Society. And where discipline is managed with a bias of opinion towards this or that party, or anyone aims to show favour against truth and justice in this or that case, a minister ought to exert himself, impartially aiming at the just and right thing without respect to either person or party. For no other kind of conduct will bear the light; but this will stand the test, and the more it is examined, it will appear the brighter. Therefore the wisdom of our discipline appears in its moderation, and justness in its proceedings, by admitting of appeals to reexamine all cases, from the lowest to our last resort of judgment; which is provided as a remedy against hasty and rash judging without duly examining into the truth and equity of what they give judgment in.

I have enlarged, as some may apprehend, too much on some heads in this treatise, which is swelled under my pen more than I expected; but I could not express my experience intelligibly to my own understanding in fewer words. For which reason I hope my readers will cast a favourable eye upon it, not being a work designed for critics, or such who are bringing all they read within the narrow bounds of their carnal reasoning and their natural comprehension, and will not admit what is not agreeable to their thoughts to be any other than fiction and enthusiastic whim. — I shall now close thus: That if we who are concerned as ministers conduct ourselves as is before advised, we shall come up pretty near to the pattern the Holy Apostle has given us: "Giving no offence in any thing, that the ministry be not blamed: But in all things *(or in every condition of life)* approving ourselves as the ministers of God, in much patience, in afflictions, in necessities, in distresses, in stripes, in imprisonments, in tumults, in labours, in watchings, in fastings; by pureness, by knowledge, by longsuffering, by kindness, by the Holy Ghost, by love unfeigned, by the Word of Truth, by the power of God, by the armour of righteousness on the right hand and on the left, by honour and dishonour, by evil report and good report: as deceivers, and yet true; as unknown, and yet well known; as dying, and, behold, we live; as chastened, and not killed; as sorrowful, yet always rejoicing; as poor, yet making many rich; as having 2 Cor 6:3-10   nothing, and yet possessing all things."

A SHORT VIEW OF THAT GREAT AND SOLEMN DUTY OF PRAYER

WHEN WE PRAY in the public assemblies or in private families of the Lord's people, we ought carefully to guard against all impertinence of expression and indecency of sounds or deportment; to prevent all which, consider well the frame of thy heart, that thee is in a meek and quiet disposition, being calm in thy mind. This will keep thee, that the heat of thy own spirit, in a mistaken blind zeal, hurry thee not too fast, without a right understanding of the ability received by the Spirit of Prayer; for the same Spirit which assisted us in the ministry will likewise in prayer, without the help of which we can perform neither as we ought. But I have observed some, by a transport of zeal (rather passion), go into a flow of words without a right understanding either of their own spirits or of the Spirit of Prayer, but in a confused manner directing their matter to the people in a way of preaching, and then to the Almighty in a way of prayer, and then returning again to the people, which has made it very tiresome, and could serve no other end than to expose the parties concerned to pity or contempt, and bring reproach on the principle they profess. Such conduct plainly demonstrates that there is want of both the Spirit and understanding so essential to the performance of this solemn duty.

Cf.
Mt 6:9-13

Our blessed Saviour, having first set the false and fictitious prayer in a true light, teaches his disciples their duty herein, saying, "After this manner therefore pray ye"; and then lays down that most beautiful and comprehensive prayer. But with how little thought, consideration, or seriousness is it frequently repeated by sundry that use it? I am fearful it is little better in many than taking the Lord's name in vain. It therefore ought to be seriously considered by all, that in using that or any other prayer, they are in some degree qualified by the Spirit so to do, whether it be in public or in private. For public prayer sometimes is adapted to beseech the Divine Majesty to confirm by his Word the various branches of doctrine that may have been before delivered, and to strengthen that faith begot by the gospel preached, and to increase vigour in the pure mind stirred up in the hearers by the inspiration of the divine Word. The royal psalmist prayed the Lord, saying, "O Lord, open thou my lips; and my mouth shall shew

Ps 51:15

forth thy praise." And when our lips are thus opened, this is the right qualification to true prayer; and it will edify and comfort the hearers who are alive to God, so that the right-minded will all say *Amen*.